"I am amazed by the richness and warmth of the text thinking that should be introduced in all teacher/pe effect of the text can be situated on different levels:

- on the 'square millimeter' of the moments with children and teachers, where listening is an ethical activity in each moment instead of a linear process to be organized in a step-by-step 'procedure';
- on an intercultural level in different countries. Davies takes us to meetings from her own neighborhood to Sweden and back;
- on an abstract level of different theoretical/philosophical backgrounds. I think no one in the world can link abstract concepts of Barad, Butler, Deleuze . . . with 'real life' realities like Bronwyn Davies is doing. While she is doing this she is opening opportunities for bringing, for example, teacher training to a level that exceeds the technical;
- on a methodological level by the introduction of the concept of 'diffraction', and challenging the concept of reflection. This is very courageous because it is like swimming against a stream full of 'reflective practitioner' slogans.

The chapters of this book can be seen as ethical-political because they offer a powerful discourse pleading for uncertainty. Identities are not fixed but flexible and nomadic. Self is seen as something that . . . has to be discovered as active (read: emergent/changing) rather than a fixed state of being."

Dr Geert Van Hove
Ghent University/Free University Amsterdam, Holland

"The book focuses on the intra-action among children and also between children and adults, professionals and educators working especially with young children. It draws attention to the important issue of how to move towards emergent listening and to anticipate ethical questions which appear in intra-actions with children. Through the analyses in different settings, the book provides a new understanding of what emergent listening requires of us, and what intra-action is, and how children, community and its materials can become continuously legitimate actors in the encounters within a community.

The well-organized introduction and interesting and profound knowledge of the studied domain gives the reader a clear picture of the studied settings. The research data is valuable in its distinctiveness, and the illuminating manner of the book gives interesting insights to life in these communities. The contribution of this book is in the thought-provoking presentation of exceptional data, depicting the multiplicity and ambivalence of the day-to-day encounters among children, and also between children and adults.

As the aim of the book is to open up, and clarify, the multiple agencies that are functioning together, it can be seen to work against the taken-for-granted presuppositions concerning the interactions between adults and children. The author's own novel conceptualizations are thorough and detailed, redefining the terms used, and opening up the concepts to make them clearly comprehensible . . . The theory supports the argument of what listening to children means, how it is generated, and how the children can be produced as legitimate political agents and subjects. These conceptualizations succeed in bringing a novel insight to theories of encounters in pedagogy . . . Studies of children always require ethical inquiry, which the author provides by opening up the studied encounters in minute detail.

There is a need for this kind of novel view in early childhood education and pedagogy. This kind of literature is scarce, and this book offers a unique and novel new opening. Professor Bronwyn Davies is a well-known and highly appreciated expert in the studies of education in Finland and in Scandinavia.

Professor Davies' thinking and theorizing is one of a kind; she has based these new ideas on her well-established and distinctive earlier thinking about the subject and its connection to the world. Nevertheless she manages to 'ascend' to different levels each time she writes, and succeeds in 'renewing' herself and her thinking in each new book. I see this book as unique in its methodological approach, as well as in its very own pedagogical approach."

Teija Rantala
University of Helsinki, Finland

"In this book we are taken on a journey, a flight, exploring possibilities of becoming communities. Davies uses encounters at a Reggio-Emilia-inspired preschool in Sweden to open wonderful possibilities for researching in ways that are not restricted and confined but mobile, intra-active and multiple. Her ways of making sense of analysis as emergent and unpredictable and, at the same time, her analysis of the contribution of Deleuze and Barad take the reader beyond the preschool to really understanding the ways we are multiple, mobile, intra-active and always becoming. This analysis makes a significant contribution to the work of preschools in particular and also to all researchers whose desire is to explore the not-yet-known.

Davies' exploration of emergent listening inspires the reader to really think about listening as relational, and as taking us to new and creative places. She uses stories/data from a collective biography workshop, a Reggio-Emilia-inspired preschool and from her own local community to analyse the complexity of *being-knowing-becoming*. This analysis really takes theorising on amazing lines of flight that can inform thinking, policy and practice about learning for years to come.

As well, she teases out ideas about anger, going almost beyond post-structuralism. Her use of Deleuze, Buddhist thought and Barad demonstrates how using a diffractive analysis might take us as practitioners and researchers to amazing places. Then her analysis of art-making with a young girl in her neighbourhood takes the reader into the personal and everyday and shows how this 'data' can be used to extend thinking through diffractive analyses. The moments of 'ah-ha' are multiple, as new ways of making sense of data, including the everyday, are made possible.

The book, finally, takes the reader to a new narrative for a well-loved story, bringing together all the new ideas in the book about agency, meaning-making, ethics, community, listening to children – and experimenting. In reading this book I am excited by the future possibilities of listening to children, learning and researching – all at the same time. It is, for the reader, a wonderful beginning."

Dr Cath Laws
Australian Catholic University, Australia

Listening to Children

Through a series of exquisite encounters with children, and through a lucid opening up of new aspects of poststructuralist theorizing, Bronwyn Davies explores new ways of thinking about and intra-acting with children.

This book carefully guides the reader through a wave of thought that turns the known into the unknown, and then slowly makes new forms of thought comprehensible, opening through all the senses a deep understanding of our embeddedness in encounters with each other and with the material world.

This book takes us into Reggio-Emilia-inspired preschools in Sweden, into the author's own community in Australia and into poignant memories of childhood, and offers the reader insights into:

- new ways of thinking about children and their communities
- the act of listening as emergent and alive
- ourselves as mobile and multiple subjects
- the importance of remaining open to the not-yet-known.

Defining research as diffractive and experimental, Davies' relationship to the teachers and pedagogues she worked with is one of co-experimentation. Her relationship with the children is one in which she explores the ways her own new thinking and being might emerge, even as old ways of thinking and being assert themselves and interfere with the unfolding of the new. She draws us into her ongoing experimentation, asking that we think hard, all the while delighting our senses with the poetry of her writing, and the stories of her encounters with children.

Bronwyn Davies is a professorial fellow at Melbourne University, Australia, and an independent scholar. Visit www.bronwyndavies.com.au for more information on Bronwyn's work.

Series Title: Contesting Early Childhood
Series Editors: Gunilla Dahlberg and Peter Moss

This groundbreaking series questions the current dominant discourses surrounding early childhood, and offers instead alternative narratives of an area that is now made up of a multitude of perspectives and debates.

The series examines the possibilities and risks arising from the accelerated development of early childhood services and policies, and illustrates how it has become increasingly steeped in regulation and control. Insightfully, this collection of books shows how early childhood services can in fact contribute to ethical and democratic practices. The authors explore new ideas taken from alternative working practices in both the Western and developing world, and from other academic disciplines such as developmental psychology. Current theories and best practice are placed in relation to the major processes of political, social, economic, cultural and technological change occurring in the world today.

Titles in the *Contesting Early Childhood* series include:

Moss (2014) *Transformative Change and Real Utopias in Early Childhood Education*

Sellers (2013) *Young Children Becoming Curriculum*

Taylor (2013) *Reconfiguring the Natures of Childhood*

Moss (2013) *Early Childhood and Compulsory Education*

Vecchi (2010) *Art and Creativity in Reggio Emilia*

Taguchi (2009) *Going Beyond the Theory/Practice Divide*

Olsson (2009) *Movement and Experimentation in Young Children's Learning*

Edmiston (2007) *Forming Ethical Identities in Early Childhood Play*

Rinaldi (2005) *In Dialogue with Reggio Emilia*

MacNaughton (2005) *Doing Foucault in Early Childhood Studies*

Penn (2005) *Unequal Childhoods*

Dahlberg and Moss (2005) *Ethics and Politics in Early Childhood*

Listening to Children

Being and becoming

Bronwyn Davies

LONDON AND NEW YORK

First published 2014
by Routledge
2 Park Square, Milton Park, Abingdon, Oxon OX14 4RN

and by Routledge
711 Third Avenue, New York, NY 10017

Routledge is an imprint of the Taylor & Francis Group, an informa business

British Library Cataloguing in Publication Data
A catalogue record for this book is available from the British Library

Library of Congress Cataloging in Publication Data
   Davies, Bronwyn, 1945–
   Listening to children : being and becoming / Bronwyn Davies.
   pages cm—(Contesting early childhood)
   1. Teacher-student relationships. 2. Reggio Emilia approach
   (Early childhood education) I. Title.
   LB1033.D38 2014
   371.102'3—dc23
   2013050500

ISBN: 978-1-138-78088-0 (hbk)
ISBN: 978-1-138-78090-3 (pbk)
ISBN: 978-1-315-77039-0 (ebk)

Typeset in Bembo
by Swales & Willis Ltd, Exeter, Devon, UK

Contents

Series editors' foreword

Gunilla Dahlberg and Peter Moss

We live today in a world under threat from a "dictatorship of no alternative" (Unger, 2005): a regime of neoliberalism with its totalizing story of the necessity of competition, calculation and individual choice enacted by a prescribed subject, *homo economicus*. This story finds expression in an education discourse devoted, as the author of this book puts it, to "the production of generic individuals whose function is to make a contribution to the market economy . . . [and a focus that] is regulatory and based on the micro-management of the production of measurable and uniform outcomes". In early childhood education, neoliberalism produces what a recent book in this series (Moss, 2014) terms the Story of Quality and High Returns, in which a combination of positivistic social science and powerful technical practice supposedly makes early childhood education into a highly profitable social investment, contributing to the exploitation of "human capital" and the creation of the flexible and compliant workforce required by globalized capital, as well as providing an antidote to the social discontents that are both a consequence of and a danger to neoliberalism's rapacious progress.

But the dictatorship of no alternative does not go uncontested. There exists a vibrant and articulate resistance movement, not just contesting neoliberalism and its educational offspring, but able to offer a wealth of other stories. Bronwyn Davies' book in this series is part of this abundance, an important addition to the Contesting Early Childhood series whose purpose is to offer "alternative narratives of an area that is now made up of a multitude of perspectives and debates".

Listening to Children is itself an "assemblage of stories", a profusion drawn from many sources: "from the Reggio-Emilia-inspired preschools I have visited in Sweden, in particular Trollet in Kalmar; from the community I live in, in Sydney, Australia; from literary sources; and from memories of childhood that I have told and written in collective biography workshops". Through these diverse stories, Bronwyn undertakes the important but difficult work of showing how "to translate philosophical concepts into practice", and by so doing maintains the constant tenor of this series: that though early childhood education today may be dominated by a particular discourse, there are alternatives

– not just being studied and written about, but actually being put to work and done in preschools and other environments where young children and adults encounter each other.

This book works with and deepens our understanding of a number of theorists, experiences and themes that have emerged in this series as playing a leading part in resisting the dominant neoliberal narrative in early childhood education and its will to manage and measure, its fixation with predictable and uniform outcomes. Bronwyn is inspired, in particular, by the theoretical perspectives and concepts of the French philosopher Gilles Deleuze. As in earlier books in this series by Liselott Mariett Olsson (2009), Hillevi Lenz Taguchi (2010) and Marg Sellers (2013), and indeed across an increasing array of education publications, Deleuze is a major presence in *Listening to Children*, his ideas and concepts opening up an amazing range of new perspectives and possibilities. Given the burgeoning interest, perhaps Foucault was right when he suggested that this might become the "Deleuzian century".

After "reading (and more recently writing with) Deleuze for over a decade now, not knowing where his often inaccessible and complex writing might take me", Bronwyn concedes that "Deleuze is a struggle", adding that it "takes time, and the concepts only work if you experience them for yourself". But the struggle has been worthwhile, for "Deleuze takes you into the not-yet-known, the not-yet-thinkable, where one must forget, and let go, in order to open up to the new". Deleuze holds out the prospect of escaping fixed positions, the already known and repetitive thinking, and refusing the urge to grasp the Other to make them into the Same; and of finding instead the joys of movement and experimentation, the excitement of the spontaneous emergence of something new and wholly unexpected. His ideas are truly transformative.

Another strong influence on Bronwyn is an exceptional education experience: the pedagogical work of the municipal schools in Reggio Emilia. These schools for young children, from the first year of life to six years of age, are the subject of books in this series by Carlina Rinaldi (2006) and Vea Vecchi (2010). But they also provide inspiration to other authors in this series and, of course, well beyond (though, sadly, it must be admitted this inspiration stops at the primary school gates, since few in the compulsory education world appear to know anything about Reggio Emilia). Her thinking in this book, Bronwyn acknowledges, has been

> deeply affected by the Reggio Emilia philosophy, which advocates listening to children as a significant part of its philosophy and practice. Being open to difference and to new thought is integral to the kind of listening that Reggio Emilia philosophy advocates. It requires practitioners capable of thinking creatively about what they are doing with children. It is a philosophy that is impacting on early childhood research and education everywhere, asking of researcher-practitioners that they work with concepts to open up new ways of seeing and being in their work with children.

As this excerpt and, indeed, the title of her book suggest, listening is a central theme in Bronwyn's writing. There is, of course, listening and listening. There is, for instance, listening as a ploy for better governing others: "we listen in order to fit what we hear into what we already know" and listening can all too easily become a thin veneer of quasi-democracy covering a will to manage and control. But there is listening as an ethical relationship based on respect for difference and the Other, "listening as continual openness to the not-yet-known", an "emergent listening" written about so eloquently by Carlina Rinaldi (2006) from Reggio Emilia, and by Bronwyn in this book:

> Listening is about being open to being affected. It is about being open to difference and, in particular, to difference in all its multiplicity as it emerges in each moment in between oneself and another. Listening is about *not* being bound by what you already know. It is life as movement. Listening to children is not just a matter of good pedagogy; encounters with others, where each is open to being affected by the other, is integral, I will suggest, to life itself . . . But more than this, it means opening up the ongoing possibility of coming to see life, and one's relation to it, in new and surprising ways.

This understanding of listening, this "emergent" listening, lies at the heart of Reggio Emilia's pedagogy: indeed, Reggio Emilia names its work "a pedagogy of listening". But such listening is neither universally understood nor desired. At odds with the desire to regulate and control inscribed in the dominant discourse espoused today by neoliberal governments, there is an "ever-present danger of turning emergent listening, and the related strategies of attention, into listening-as-usual, that is, into, repetitive listening, not requiring any thought, and serving to reiterate that which is already known".

Other related themes in the book include the importance of encounter, especially with difference; being open to affect and being affected by others; not being bound by what we already know and pre-existing categories; the importance of new thought, Deleuze's "lines of flight", and of movement and experimentation; evolving, becoming and being in-between (not at all to be confused with "development"); and the centrality of ethics. In Bronwyn's words, "[t]he ethics of my story gives primacy to movement, to the eruption of the new, while at the same time not letting go of the fact that any new idea must not come into existence at the expense of other beings, and without letting go of a commitment to the multiplicity of truths as a value". Ethics, too, is closely bound up with listening, and doing so in ways that express an "openness to emergent difference in the other and in oneself, and openness to the not-yet-known . . . [and] for that which cannot yet be said".

In its exploration of the concept of "community", the book also contributes in important ways to deepening our understanding of the potentiality of the school, whether for young or older children. For Bronwyn, a community provides the possibility of "ongoing encounters among coexisting multiplic-ities" and for "emergent listening". But the realization of such potentiality requires certain conditions. Not least, we must open ourselves to being sur-prised by such encounters, to the not-yet-known and to being affected by the other – "with all the riskiness that that might entail".

So communities, including schools, are "always emergent, experimental spaces in which a multiplicity of possibilities for thinking and doing coexist . . . They are emergent assemblages with multiple entry points, and multiple, often opposing lines of force". A community is always "relational, plural, and emer-gent . . . a place where multiple distinct pathways coexist, and co-implicate each other". The school-as-community so understood is a place of possibility, of "rich and infinite variability", of and . . . and . . . and. The implications for education of this way of conceptualizing the school are immense, wonderful – and deeply threatening to the dominant educational discourse, saturated as it is by the narrow, calculative and controlling spirit of neoliberalism.

For that discourse has a very different understanding of schools – utilitarian, grey and soul destroying. The school is seen as a place of discipline and control, of thinking in fixed and categorical terms, a place driven by "the stifling ten-dency of the will-to-order and to predictability", and dedicated to the repro-duction of knowledge and the production of predetermined outcomes through the application of a wide range of powerful human technologies made available to managers in today's "societies of control" (another prescient concept from Deleuze (1992)). As Bronwyn observes:

> It suits our current neoliberal governments, in particular, to think of every-one in a community as having measurable and manipulable characteristics, and to this end, to think of any community and its members as entities, or objects, that can be pinned down, categorized, and made predictable.

This impoverished, static but dominant way of thinking and viewing the world makes the life-affirming early childhood education in places like the Reggio Emilia municipal schools and Trollet preschool all the more important. But it also puts that education at risk. Bronwyn shares our concerns about the possibility of neoliberalism undermining such important pedagogical work, pedagogical work which (along with this and other books in the series) poses such a threat to the dictatorship of no alternative – because it shows so vividly that there are alternatives and, worse, that these alternatives have the power to affect, enthuse and inspire because they offer the prospect that we can, in Deleuze's words, believe in the world again.

A final thought provoked by this book. Reggio Emilia's pedagogical project, its 50 years of work to create a new public education, has been encoun-tered by many others in many other countries, not least in Sweden where preschools and preschool teachers have been in dialogue with Reggio for decades. The result has been the evolution of a Swedish network of

Reggio-inspired preschools, which has grown out of the experimental work that was carried out in the 1990s in the practice-oriented research project *Early Childhood Pedagogy in a Changing World* (for a description and discussion of this Stockholm project, see Chapter 7 in Dahlberg *et al.*, 2013). This network, and further pedagogical work inspired by the dialogue with Reggio, has since been supported by the Reggio Emilia Institute in Stockholm and by research carried out at Stockholm University (formerly the Stockholm Institute of Education).

The Swedish preschools that Bronwyn recounts in this book, one of which she has been returning to for five years, are part of this Reggio network and vividly demonstrate the rich results of this encounter between two different cultures. For the pedagogical work that Bronwyn witnesses in these preschools is clearly very special:

> There I have met wonderful teachers, pedagogues and children, who have engaged with me in opening up new thoughts and new ways of being in the world. That experimental openness to engaging with the other is integral to the kind of listening that I want to explore here in this book . . . When they invited me to participate in their community, they invited me to become part of their ongoing experimentation . . . To be welcomed into Reggio-Emilia-inspired communities is to be welcomed as a potential catalyst for new thought – not as someone who brings superior (or inferior) knowledge from outside, but as someone who will enter into that ongoing emergent project of discovery.

This is not the first example in this series of the capacity of Swedish preschools and their teachers to work with inspiration from Reggio Emilia, adopting a pedagogy of listening, a practice of documentation and an attitude of movement and experimentation (see also Dahlberg and Moss, 2005; Olsson, 2009; Moss, 2014). But reflect a moment on this phenomenon. The way Sweden organizes its early childhood education is commendable, with a fully integrated system offering preschools that combine care, learning and upbringing as an entitlement to all children from twelve months to six years of age and staffed by a well-educated workforce of preschool teachers. But what is equally impressive is the supportive milieu that this system provides for alternative pedagogical approaches, for educators wanting to work with new theoretical perspectives, for thinking creatively, for movement and experimentation.

This system, it should be noted, is mainly run by municipalities, democratically elected local authorities. It is a public system (like Reggio's schools), which views early childhood education as a common good and that until now has struggled to stand in defiance of neoliberalism's dogma of markets and privatization. It combines a coherent framework of provision with conditions that seem to favour pedagogical diversity, border crossing and experimentation. Bronwyn's book, therefore, confronts us with important questions that are both pedagogical and political and asks us to adopt perspectives that are both local and systemic.

But this book is not just about Reggio Emilia and Sweden, or exclusively about early childhood education. It will take you to many other places, including zen buddhism, fairy tales, the neighbourhood where Bronwyn lives and her friendship with young Clementine and their shared love of art. We think you will enjoy the journey.

References

Dahlberg, G. and Moss, P. (2005) *Ethics and Politics in Early Childhood Education*. London: Routledge.

Dahlberg, G., Moss, P. and Pence, A. (2013) *Beyond Quality in Early Childhood Education and Care: Languages of evaluation* (3rd edn). London: Routledge.

Deleuze, G. (1992) "Postscript on the societies of control". *October* 59: 3–7.

Lenz Taguchi, H. (2010) *Going Beyond the Theory/Practice Divide in Early Childhood Education: Introducing an intra-active pedagogy*. London: Routledge.

Moss, P. (2014) *Transformative Change and Real Utopias in Early Childhood Education: A story of democracy, experimentation and potentiality*. London: Routledge.

Olsson, L. M. (2009) *Movement and Experimentation in Young Children's Learning: Deleuze and Felix Guattari in early childhood education*. London: Routledge.

Rinaldi, C. (2006) *In Dialogue with Reggio Emilia: Listening, researching and learning*. London: Routledge.

Sellers, M. (2013) *Young Children Becoming Curriculum: Deleuze, Te Whāriki and curricular understandings*. London: Routledge.

Unger, R. M. (2005) *What Should the Left Propose?* London: Verso.

Vecchi, V. (2010) *Art and Creativity in Reggio Emilia: Exploring the role and potential of ateliers in early childhood education*. London: Routledge.

Acknowledgements

I would like to thank the wonderful children from Trollet in Kalmar and the extraordinary teachers and pedagogues who work with them. In particular I would like to thank Christina Nilsson and Birgitta Kennedy who hosted and facilitated my annual visits to Trollet. Harold Gothson of the Reggio Emilia Institutet in Sweden was also especially encouraging and supportive of my work, and to him I give my very warm thanks. My thanks, too, to the teachers and pedagogues at each of the other Swedish Reggio-Emilia-inspired preschools that I visited during this study, including, in particular, Karin Alvernick at HallonEtt in Jönköping.

Closer to home, I would like to thank, from the bottom of my heart, the members of my own community; in particular, Claudia and Matt Bowman and their beloved daughter Clementine. Clementine's paintings and our time spent together have been vital.

Dan Davies created the illustrations for Plates 17 and 18. For those illustrations and for his open-hearted wisdom, my special thanks.

To my friends and colleagues, who have read and responded to various versions of this writing since it began, I could not have engaged in this work without the onto-epistemological space of encounter that you make possible, in which new thought has been able to unfold itself; nor could I have proceeded without the heart-space you so generously offer me, in which the always emergent process of becoming is made possible.

Thanks too to the staff of Petrol, the café next door, where many of the new thoughts, and much of this writing, took place.

Papers and books I have published that are reproduced here in part, and in modified form, include:

Davies, B. (2014) "The affective flows of art-making". *Bank Street Occasional Papers*.
Davies, B. (2014) "Reading anger in early childhood intra-actions: A diffractive analysis". *Qualitative Inquiry* 20(7), first published on 10 April 2014 as doi: 10.1177/1077800414530256.
Davies, B. (2014) "A feminist line of flight with the Fairy Who Wouldn't Fly". In E. Söderberg, M. Österlund and B. Formark (eds), *Fliktion. Perspektiv på flickan i fiktionen*. Universus Academic Press: Malmo, pp. 293–307.

Davies, B. (2011) "Intersections between Zen Buddhism and Deleuzian philosophy". *Psyke and Logos* 32(1): 28–45.

Davies, B. (2011) "Open listening: Creative evolution in early childhood settings". *International Journal of Early Childhood* 43(2): 119–132.

Davies, B. (2011) "Listening: A radical pedagogy". In S. Fahlgren (ed.), *Challenging Gender: Normalization and beyond*. Mid-Sweden University, Sundsval: Forum for genusvetenskap, pp. 107–120.

Davies, B. (2010) "The implications for qualitative research methodology of the struggle between the individualized subject of phenomenology and the emergent multiplicities of the poststructuralist subject: The problem of agency". *Reconceptualizing Educational Research Methodology* 1(1): 54–68.

Davies, B. (2009) Forskolan – en demokratisk tankesmedja? *Modern Barndom* 1(9): 25–27.

O'Harris, P. (retold by Bronwyn Davies) (2014) *The Fairy Who Wouldn't Fly*. Canberra: Australian National Library.

Chapter 1

Children and community

My inspiration for this book about listening to children has come from Reggio-Emilia-inspired preschools in Sweden. There I have met wonderful teachers, pedagogues and children, who have engaged with me in opening up new thoughts and new ways of being in the world. That experimental openness to engaging with the other is integral to the kind of listening that I want to explore here in this book. Listening is about being open to being affected. It is about being open to difference and, in particular, to difference in all its multiplicity as it emerges in each moment in between oneself and another. Listening is about *not* being bound by what you already know. It is life as movement. Listening to children is not just a matter of good pedagogy; encounters with others, where each is open to being affected by the other, is integral, I will suggest, to life itself.

My emphasis on openness to becoming different in one's encounters with others does not run against or deny the very specificity of each person, or the longing each one of us has to be recognized in that specificity. Rather, I am suggesting that the very specificity of each individual is *mobile* and *intra-active*; in each encounter we are affected by the other (Lenz Taguchi, 2010). Our capacity to enter into encounters, to re-compose ourselves, to be affected, *enhances* our specificity and *expands* our capacity for thought and for action (Dahlberg and Moss, 2005).

To open out this space of inquiry about what listening to children might be and become, I draw stories from a number of sources: from the Reggio-Emilia-inspired preschools I have visited in Sweden, in particular Trollet in Kalmar; from the community I live in, in Sydney, Australia; from literary sources; and from memories of childhood that I have told and written in collective biography workshops (Davies and Gannon, 2006). In this first chapter I will ponder the concept and practice of community, drawing on stories from Trollet. In the second chapter I will develop the concept of emergent listening, with stories from a number of places, including my own community. The third chapter extends the analysis into the question of identity versus intra-active becoming, drawing on one of my own collective biography stories, returning to Trollet, then back to my own community. The fourth chapter focuses on conflicting lines of force and analyses the affect of anger as it emerges between two boys at Trollet, and introduces some zen buddhist concepts into the mix. The fifth chapter brings the conceptual work in the first four chapters into my own everyday practice through an exploration of the artwork that I have done over a number of years with Clementine, a child in my community. The final chapter explores the way in which the analytic work of the chapters so far can be used to write a children's story about listening.

Methodological note: Diffraction as concept and practice

My research methodology is what I call, after Barad (2007), a diffractive methodology (see also Hultman and Lenz Taguchi, 2010). The concept of diffraction replaces the more usual concept and practice in qualitative research of reflexivity. Reflection, or reflexivity, is implicitly based on the phenomenon of a pattern of light that reflects an actual object or entity. The task of the reflexive researcher, Barad suggests, is akin to the task of quantitative researchers, in that it seeks to *represent* what is already there, independent of the researcher's gaze. Such representation is doubly problematic; not only does it act as a conservative force, but it obscures the fact that the object of the reflexive gaze can never simply be an object capable of being pinned down (Davies *et al.*, 2004; Lenz Taguchi, 2012; Lenz Taguchi and Palmer, 2013). As Barad observes, on the basis of physics experiments with light: "Reflection is insufficient; intervention is the key" (2007: 50). Diffraction does not reflect an image of what is already there, but is actually involved in its ongoing production.

We are so used to using reflection and reflexivity as the primary conceptual and practical analytic tools of qualitative research, that shifting to diffraction as metaphor and practice makes for a significant interference in thinking-as-usual. Whereas reflection and reflexivity might document *difference*, diffraction is itself the process whereby a *difference is made*:

> diffraction does not fix what is the object and what is the subject in advance, and so, unlike methods of reading one text or set of ideas against another where one set serves as a fixed frame of reference, diffraction involves reading insights through one another in ways that help illuminate differences as they emerge: how different differences get made, what gets excluded, and how these exclusions matter.
>
> (Barad, 2007: 30)

An article of faith in positivist research is that the research itself must not make a difference, since its findings must reveal what always already exists. Barad (2007) argues that the technologies of observation not only cannot be separated from what is observed, but they will always be intra-acting with (affecting and interfering with) the reality that is observed and experimented with. What a diffractive methodology does is to track the interference patterns, and discover from them the ongoing diffractive processes through which the world creates itself. A diffractive approach thus opens an onto-epistemological space of *encounter*.

The concept of encounter focuses attention on the ongoing intra-active processes through which ~~subjects~~ come into being. The line through the word subjects, here, interferes with the tendency that our language has to invoke entities which it then takes to be real, fixing them in place through ways of speaking – or modes of enunciation. The line through the word seeks to erase that fixity. The ~~subject~~ does exist, but its existence is more mobile, intra-active and multiple than our modes of enunciation normally suggest. The diffractive researcher's task, then, is not to tell of something that exists independent of the research encounter, but to open up an immanent truth – to access that which is becoming true, ontologically *and* epistemologically, in the moment of the research encounter. A research encounter in this sense is experimental – the researcher does not know in advance what onto-epistemological knowledge will emerge from it (Hultman and Lenz Taguchi, 2010; Lenz Taguchi, 2012).

Diffraction, as a concept for thinking about the generation of data or the analytic work with that data, does not try to fix those processes so that they can be turned into a methodic set of steps to be followed. Rather, it opens the possibility of seeing how something different comes to matter, not only in the world that we observe, but also in our research practice:

> So while it is true that diffraction apparatuses [of physics] measure the effects of difference, even more profoundly they highlight, exhibit, and make evident the entangled structure of the changing and contingent ontology of the world, including the ontology of knowing. In fact, diffraction not only brings the reality of entanglements to light, it is itself an entangled phenomenon.
>
> (Barad, 2007: 73)

Ideas, concepts and practices, like particles of light, ripples on a pond, or criss-crossing waves on the ocean, affect each other – they interfere with each other. Ideas and matter similarly affect each other. And just as ripples and waves and drops of foam do not exist without the body of water, or the wind, or the other matter they encounter (stones, sand, rocks, human bodies . . .), we, as social science researchers, are part of, and encounter, already entangled matter and meanings that affect us, and that we affect, in an ongoing, always changing set of movements.

Each action we engage in and each interpretation is, therefore, an ethical matter and mattering. When something comes to matter, when it actively changes the way things are and are perceived to be, both the ontology of bodies (our own and others'), and the meanings made of what happens, are affected:

"Mattering is simultaneously a matter of substance and significance" (Barad, 2007: 3).

Taking up a diffractive methodology, I experience a shift from the desire to produce lucid documentation and analysis to the desire to listen intently to the multi-directional, minutely detailed patterns of interference. Interference is understood here not as an undesirable negative, but as the nature of existence. Life itself is not a matter of separate self-same entities (concepts, affects, percepts, actions, identities) but of movement within and among them. I am, as researcher, inextricably part of those movements. Everything I do/think matters in some way. This is the ethical dimension. I cannot leave my ethical responsibility out, insofar as my research is actively engaged, whether I realize it or not, in mattering – in making a difference.

For the purposes of writing this book I cannot simply reflect on my analytic practice as if it were an observable entity. It is a series of movements, affected already by the choice to see them as diffractive, and to think about them diffractively. And if analysis is a set of encounters among meaning, matter and ethics, as Barad suggests, those encounters are always already *affecting* and being affected by the meanings and mattering that I am analysing. This should not be read as a weakness of qualitative work, but rather, in Barad's terms, a means of getting closer to the "fundamental constituents that make up the world" (Barad, 2007: 72). The stories I tell and the analytic work I do with them are an entanglement of intra-acting encounters, and the very act of writing about them is one further element in a complex array of entangled movements.

As Berlant observes, diffractive analysis provokes a "letting go of 'archaic attachments' to often hierarchical 'cultural traditions'", and it opens up a "space of sociality that listens, is receptive, and calls for theory", that asks, further, that we be open to those who we encounter, and are open to being changed by each encounter. It asks that we "[b]ecome a poet of the episode, the elision, the ellipsis" (Berlant, 2010: 103).

Those encounters are with human others, but also non-human others, as in the following encounter:

> Diary entry: Arriving in unexpected places. September 2011.
> As we flew toward Copenhagen there was a spectacular storm cloud, magnificent to see, clouds banked up high, huge white puffs with dark blue edges and swathes of dark blue violet behind. We couldn't land and diverted to Malmo in Sweden, where the storm followed us. The pilots had planned to take us to Copenhagen when the storm passed but they found, as we sat there on the tarmac, that their allowable time in the cockpit was up. They could not take us back to Copenhagen. It was a public holiday. There were no pilots in Malmo who could fly this plane. Malmo airport did not have the facilities to offload us. Thus stranded on the tarmac in Malmo at the end of a 24-hour flight, there was plenty of time to ponder what it might mean to arrive somewhere, to get out pencil and paper and begin to write.

What encounters, I wonder, will I have in the next 6 weeks of travel? . . .

Even as one anticipates the space of talking to someone new, something surprising may happen. The anticipation of the virtual other, and then the presence of the actual other, already makes an opening. But the opening may produce no more than a dull thud and a loss – or it may be a sudden spark in which the previously unknowable/unsayable becomes clearly present. Everything shifts. A fleeting moment, barely able to be traced, but it leaves its trace somehow, and the idea, not previously thinkable, emerges. Such encounters are also possible between oneself and a book – even a book one writes oneself (as Barad expresses it), or a paper. Or between two different papers one is writing. Or oneself and a magnificent storm cloud, which evokes a rush of writing. The agency of the cloud – it can force the plane off its course, and push me into getting out my pencil and beginning to write.

I hadn't done any work on this trip, other than the emotional work of transferring myself from one hemisphere to the other, letting go of the secure web of life at home and opening up for the as-yet-unknown. Opening up to encounters is what thought needs – to unsettle it, to disturb it, to move it.

In a diffractive analysis "the researcher" is not the only agent. Storm clouds, regulations that pilots must abide by, friends, colleagues, the children observed in the preschool, books, all are actively interfering with my thought processes. My thought processes are agentic as well, working with the cloud, the pilots, the anticipated meetings, the pencil and the paper. Each is an overlapping wave, or ripple, or speck of foam on the ocean of research (Hultman and Lenz Taguchi, 2010).

The analysis I engage in here, then, cannot be a linear process with a clear beginning and end. The analysis *interferes* with the research problem and the questions being asked, and the questions interfere with the analysis. The analysis is emergent and unpredictable, a series of encounters with the new. It is hard, demanding work, requiring the capacity to let go of the already-known, and of tired clichés and explanations – archaic attachments. It involves hard epistemological and ontological work to enable the not-yet-known to emerge in the spaces of encounter – not just on my part, but on the part of the reader as well.

The concept and practice of community

If encounters with others lie at the heart of listening – and of life itself – then the community that holds and enfolds those encounters seems a good place to begin this exploration of listening to children. I begin by introducing some of the key philosophical concepts that I will draw on throughout the book, then mobilize them here to open up this space of thinking about the concept and practice of community. I will then turn to stories of children in one particular community, Trollet, a Reggio-Emilia-inspired preschool in the city of Kalmar on the south-east coast of Sweden.

The Reggio Emilia philosophy is specifically "community" oriented, regularly bringing people in from the city to interact with the children, and regularly taking the children on excursions outside the borders of the preschool (Rinaldi, 2006). It also holds openness to difference as an important value. My task here, however, is not to engage in an exposition of the Reggio Emilia philosophy, though my thinking about community is informed by it. Nor do I use my observations from Trollet as an exemplar of how a community *should* be. It is not a moral or a managerial argument I am interested in here. What I have learned from my visits to Trollet over the last five years, through my encounters with the children and their teachers and pedagogues, is about the daily *doing* of community, a doing that is emergent in ongoing encounters, a doing that cannot be mandated through moralism, or through regulations.

The stories I have chosen show children intra-acting with adults and with other children, engaging in dialogue, experimenting, and composing themselves in multiple heterogeneous encounters. They show children with power and agency, children as ethical subjects, and children listening in ways that enable the not-yet-known to emerge. I argue that it is through this mutual engagement of children with each other, with adults, and with their material environment that their always-emergent community is accomplished. I attend to these stories in minute detail, in their materiality, in their affect and emotion, in order to make visible the *mobility* of intra-action. What I hope to assemble here is an insight into community, not as an entity, but as ongoing encounters among coexisting multiplicities. Community is emergent, I will suggest, in each successive *intra-active* moment, where "intra-action" refers to more than interaction (a meeting of two pre-existing entities); it is an encounter where each participant affects, and is open to being affected by, the other (Barad, 2007; Lenz Taguchi, 2010).

My approach to the concept of community, then, is not as a geographically determined population that can be represented in demographic terms. Nor is my primary interest in structural forces. There are many external structuring forces at play that affect any community, making it in some important sense recognizably and continuously itself. Funding models and government policy play a large part in this, as do a society's beliefs and practices concerning differences such as gender, race, class, and, in this context in particular, the difference between adults and children. It would be a mistake, though, to imagine that a community is a *result* of those external forces. It is *affected* by those striating forces, but as Bergson (1998) makes clear, those striating forces are themselves movements that create no more than an illusion of a stable entity. Communities are always emergent, experimental spaces in which a multiplicity of possibilities for thinking and doing coexist. They are emergent assemblages with multiple entry points, and multiple, often opposing lines of force (Barad, 2007; Deleuze and Guattari, 1987).

Community as encounters in an always-evolving story

The tendency to think of communities as more or less stable and mono-cultural is not just a result of a failure to see their actual heterogeneity and movement. There is a tendency we all have to think in terms of categories and of entities that fit into those ready-made categories. Bergson (1998: 48) is scathing about this tendency in scientists:

> Our reason, incorrigibly presumptuous, imagines itself possessed . . . of all the essential elements of the knowledge of truth. Even where it confesses that it does not know the object presented to it, it believes that its ignorance consists only in not knowing which one of its time-honoured categories suits the new object. In what drawer, ready to open, shall we put it? In what garment, already cut out, shall we clothe it? Is it this, or that, or the other thing? And "this," and "that," and "the other thing" are always something already conceived, already known.

It suits our current neoliberal governments, in particular, to think of everyone in a community as having measurable and manipulable characteristics, and to this end, to think of any community and its members as entities, or objects, that can be pinned down, categorized, and made predictable. This tendency to think in fixed, categorical terms Bergson describes as *a line of descent*, a mode of thought that can happen instantaneously and without effort. If, however, we resist this temptation, and open ourselves up to the not-yet-known, we begin to be able to see the rich and infinite variability of any community; we open ourselves up to being surprised by the encounters that take place within those communities. Such openness gives rise to what Bergson calls *a line of ascent*:

> The universe *endures*. The more we study the nature of time, the more we shall comprehend that duration means invention, the creation of forms, the continual elaboration of the absolutely new . . . [I]n the universe itself two opposite movements are to be distinguished . . . The first [descent] only unwinds a roll ready prepared. In principle, it might be accomplished almost instantaneously, like releasing a spring. But the ascending movement, which corresponds to an inner work of ripening or creating, *endures* essentially, and imposes its rhythm on the first, which is inseparable from it.
>
> (Bergson, 1998: 11)

The lines of ascent and descent are not mutually exclusive lines of force and they cannot simply be mapped onto binaries such as good/bad, old/new.

They continually affect each other and they depend on each other. Lines of descent may foreclose the emergence of new thought, but they may also create a coherent space in which the new can emerge. Lines of ascent – or, in Deleuzian terms, lines of flight – are life-giving and powerful, but they are not always good and may sometimes be sad and even dangerous: "When a body 'encounters' another body, or an idea another idea, it happens that the two relations sometimes combine to form a more powerful whole, and sometimes one decomposes the other, destroying the cohesion of its parts" (Deleuze, 1988: 19). Lines of ascent are capable of generating great joy, but also "singular despair" (Deleuze and Guattari, 1987: 205).

Each of us, adults and children, is constantly in search of encounters that make us more powerful, more able to act effectively in the world, more capable of joy. Powerful alliances within communities are a source of such joy. But those alliances may also, sometimes, be harmful both to ourselves and to others. What is good is not necessarily good for all time, or all people. The decomposition of an alliance, or a communal set of practices, is not always wrong or bad. A usual way of thinking, or a usual practice, or striated way of being, may be urgently in need of having its cohesion decomposed in order to make space for a new line of flight, a new possibility of being. Powerful alliances that increase energy and joy are life-giving, but if they become sedimented and exclusive, and can tolerate only their own fixed point of view, they may become a stifling line of force.

Sometimes communities develop a single view of what is good, which becomes dominant and is cemented into community practice, becoming a forceful line of descent. When the good and the necessary can no longer be separated, thought becomes redundant. The line of descent is instantaneous.

Badiou argues that it is of paramount importance in a community that we do not collapse our understanding of the good and the necessary into each other. Where they are not kept separate, we are each reduced to becoming mere sophists – a sophist being, according to Plato, "the one who cannot see 'the extent to which the nature of the good and the nature of the necessary differ'" (Badiou, 2008: 150). If what we must necessarily become, and what is understood as good, become one and the same, debate about what is good is pointless. And if we legislate or otherwise dictate how everyone should think in their pursuit of the good – as neoliberal governments, globally, are fond of doing – we reduce each participant to being one whose beliefs and actions are already decided in uniform striations, that is, repeated institutionalized, authorized ways of being and knowing. Once there is no point in thinking about what we do and why we do it, we are at risk of becoming sophists, beings without the capacity to have any effect, and thus without energy, without joy, and without need of thought. Fortunately, for most who are likely to read this book, it is only totalitarian governments or fanatical religious leaders who seal absolutely the notion of the good inside what is deemed to be necessary.

If the members of any community, and in this case a preschool community, are to have agency – that is, the power to engage with others in ways that open up the capacity for thought and being – they cannot be bound, mind and body, by an overriding or closed set of rules and definitions dictated by powerful alliances, whether those be from government or from groups within the community itself. While each one of us might harbour a desire to have our own truths become the only truths, it is important to recognize that when truths become unquestionable, dialogue is suffocated; and it is dialogue among the children, among the teachers, and among teachers, children and parents, that enables each being, in their specificity, to make a "deep contribution" to the always-evolving story of their community (Rinaldi, 2006: 190). That deep contribution cannot be made-to-order through an orchestrated assent to the already-known.

The communal space of a preschool can be characterized in terms of Massey's three propositions about the nature of space:

> *First* . . . [a community space is] the product of interrelations; as constituted through interactions, from the immensity of the global to the intimately tiny . . . *Second* . . . [it is] the sphere of the possibility of the existence of multiplicity in the sense of contemporaneous plurality . . . the sphere in which distinct trajectories co-exist; as the sphere of coexisting heterogeneity . . . *Third* . . . [it is] always under construction . . . It is never finished; never closed. Perhaps we could imagine space as the simultaneity of stories so far.
>
> (Massey, 2005: 9)

A community, I suggest, with Massey, is always relational, plural, and emergent. It is a place where multiple distinct pathways coexist, and co-implicate each other. Continuous becoming is "the nature of our being" (Massey, 2005: 21). Each of us is a multiplicity in connection with other multiplicities, even where those multiplicities contain, as they inevitably do, opposing lines of force.

The self as emergent multiplicities

Multiplicities do not refer here to discrete entities existing side-by-side or even bouncing off each other, but beings that "continually transform themselves into each other, cross over into each other . . . [so that] becoming and multiplicity are the same thing" (Deleuze and Guattari, 1987: 249). We are each, like communities, produced through intra-actions; we are multiplicities, always in process of becoming other than we were before: "the self is a threshold, a door, a becoming between two. Each multiplicity is defined by a borderline . . . but there is a string of borderlines, a continuous line of borderlines (*fiber*) following which the multiplicity changes. And at each threshold or door, a new pact?" (Deleuze and Guattari, 1987: 249). Each movement across a threshold, between one and another, potentially contributes to the creative evolutionary force of each one, and of the community as a whole.

Thresholds are not only present in our encounters with human others (Davies and Gannon, 2009; Somerville *et al.*, 2011). We are, in Wilson's words, ontologically co-implicated not only with humans, but with animals as well as with "plants, rocks, and emotions" (Wilson, 2004: 69). The evolution of life, she observes, is "radically heterogeneous; certainly it is biological, but it is also psychological, cultural, geological, oceanic, and meteorological" (Wilson, 2004: 69). Our being emerges in relation to human, non-human and earth others – to a ray of light on water, for example, a tree glowing green in the late afternoon light, a breeze, the sound of laughter, a cold block of clay, a juicy orange, the smell of lunch cooking, a smile, the feeling of the air as you fly through it, a friend's hand in yours. Each joyful encounter with another is what Deleuze calls a *haecceity*, an immersion in the present moment that "moves the soul" (Deleuze, 1990: 140). An encounter is an intensity, a becoming that takes you outside the habitual practices of the already-known; it is intra-active, and corresponds to the power to affect and be affected (Deleuze and Parnet, 1987).

Being open, and being vulnerable to being affected by the other, is how we accomplish our humanity; it is how the communities, of which we are part, create and re-create themselves. We are not separate from the encounters that make up the community but, rather, emergent *with* them.

The co-implication of matter, meaning and ethics

What I want to turn to now, in this last section before I come to the stories of the children, is the inseparability and mutual dependence of meaning, matter, and ethics. Barad (2007) argues that the *study of matter* cannot actually take place in isolation either from the conceptual apparatus we bring to bear on it, or from the ethical implications of what we do to and with the matter of ourselves, the matter of each other, and of the places we live in. Each moment matters, each moment is both material and has ethical implications. Individuals and striations do not exist independently of people who think and speak and act with them, but in the emergent and multiple encounters through which individuals and communities *engage in mattering*.

Just so, ethics cannot just be a matter of separate individuals following a set of rules (where the necessary and the good are collapsed into one another). Ethical practice, as both Barad and Deleuze define it, requires thought – and it is intra-active. As Deleuze points out, "The best society, then, will be one that exempts the power of thinking from the obligation to obey, and takes care, in its own interest, not to subject thought to the rule of the state, which only applies to actions. As long as thought is free, hence vital, nothing is compromised" (1988: 4). Similarly, ethics, as Barad defines it, is a matter of questioning what is being made to matter and how that mattering affects what it is possible to do and to think. Ethics is emergent in the intra-active encounters in which knowing, being, and doing (epistemology, ontology, and ethics) are inextricably entangled (Barad, 2007).

The ways in which we affect each other, and are affected, cannot be separated from thought any more than it can be separated from bodies. Thought and action are mutually entangled, just as individual beings, who know and who act, are mutually entangled. This mutual entanglement does not absolve one from ethical responsibility. Quite the reverse: paying attention to the ways in which thought and action affect others makes each individual all the more responsible for the impact of their words and actions.

So, on the one hand, individual beings are always being subjected to pre-existing, institutionalized striations and modes of enunciation. On the other, they become subjects through the lines of force that escape those striations, in moments of *haecceity* or grace. These contrary forces, in many versions of community-making throughout history, have been collapsed into one another, the necessary and the good being defined as the same thing, such that the rules and striations, the structuring forces, become what every good person must desire. Communities are thus rendered finite, limiting, and even reducing, the potential and diversity of life within them. When contemplating the strength of this tendency to limit and constrain multiplicity, Badiou even doubts that "community" can be made to stand for such complex life forces: against this "ontological infinity of situations . . . Community seems to me unable to stand as the name for this processing of the infinite" (2008: 172).

Yet it is also true that communities cannot exist without some striations, and will always tend toward re-striating and re-territorializing both action and thought, as powerful alliances form, and re-form (Bergson, 1998; Deleuze and Guattari, 1987). *At the same time*, a community's power to endure comes from multiplicity, from encounters, from an always-emergent openness to the not-yet-known.

To escape the stifling tendency of the will-to-order and to predictability, Reggio Emilia philosophy makes the valuing of difference a primary value, along with being open to the emergence of the not-yet-thought in oneself and another (Ceppi and Zini, 1998). The capacity and willingness to be open to the other, in all his or her difference, is crucial, not only to the capacity of a community to endure, but to the constitution of that community as an ethical place: "When you consider others as part of your identity, then their different, sometimes divergent, theories and opinions are seen as a resource. The awareness of the value of these differences and of having dialogue among them increases" (Rinaldi, 2006: 206).

Ethical practice in this sense is not so much tied up with regulation and repetition (though it is partly that), but with the practice of listening for that which cannot yet be said:

to listen to Thought, to think beside each other and beside ourselves, is to explore an open network of obligations that keeps the question of meaning open as a locus of debate. Doing justice to Thought, listening to our interlocutors, means trying to hear that which cannot be said but which tries to make itself heard.

(Readings, 1996: 165)

Opening up the not-yet-known through dialogue, and through the careful listening that is involved in keeping meaning open, relies, in Reggio-Emilia-inspired preschools, on recognition of the "one hundred languages" that we share with children. The concept of a hundred languages is not only a way of crediting children and adults with multiple communicative potentials: "it is a declaration of the equal dignity and importance of *all* languages, not only writing, reading and counting . . . for the construction of knowledge" (Rinaldi, 2006: 175).

Rinaldi argues that children are extraordinary listeners – and that we, as adults, can learn from them how to engage in reciprocal listening. We can learn from children, she says, to "'listen' to life in all its facets, listen to others with generosity, quickly perceive how the act of listening is an essential act of communication" (Rinaldi, 2006: 116). Children open themselves up in multiple ways to new possibilities, and in doing so make the very basis of an ethical community possible.

Participation in an ethical community serves to enhance the specificity of each child, and at the same time, to enhance each specific child's capacity to actively participate in the making of community in all its emergent multiplicity. Communities, then, are emergent mattering, engaged, in Barad's terms, in bringing forth new worlds, engaged in reconfiguring the world. A community is not so much a place, or a finite group of people, but a way of mattering, a way of engaging with the world, and of re-configuring that world as a place where self and other matter, and make a difference, to each other and with each other.

So now to the stories from Trollet, to see how these ideas might play out in the moment-by-moment intra-actions of life in one preschool community.

Acts of listening/becoming-community

The teachers and pedagogues I encountered at Trollet, over the five years of my visits there, were scientists in the sense that Massey defines that term – where science is not a representation of what is imagined to be already there, but experimentation. When they invited me to participate in their community, they invited me to become part of their ongoing experimentation, where science is an element in a continuous production; a part of it all, and itself constantly becoming. This is a position which rejects a strict separation between world and text and which understands scientific activity as being just that – an activity, a practice, an embedded engagement *in* the world of which it is part. Not representation but experimentation.

(Massey, 2005: 28)

To be welcomed into Reggio-Emilia-inspired communities is to be welcomed as a potential catalyst for new thought – not as someone who brings superior (or inferior) knowledge from outside, but as someone who will enter into that ongoing emergent project of discovery.

Despite my lack of Swedish I immediately felt at home at Trollet. I was deeply intrigued by what new thoughts and ways of being I might find myself part of. Our encounters were, in Massey's sense, experimental, where each participant recognized and respected the other "in a situation of mutual implication", an "imaginative space of engagement", where each was emergent *in relation* to the other (Massey, 2005: 69). In Rinaldi's terms, we engaged in dialogue, entering "a process of transformation where you lose absolutely the possibility of controlling the final result" (Rinaldi, 2006: 184). That willingness to make oneself vulnerable to the thought that is yet to emerge, opens us up to dialogue with children; "the child's search for meaning in life pushes you, if you dialogue with him, into the universe" (Rinaldi, 2006: 185).

The Trollet site has a beautiful garden, with many old trees, huge round rocks – many places to hide, and places to play. The school building has at its centre a large, light piazza which functions like the public square in an Italian town. In the piazza people meet and talk, and plan, and eat, and play together, and there are long-term collaborative art projects going on. One side of the piazza has glass walls revealing a beautiful courtyard with a fountain at its centre. Each of the classrooms has glass walls opening onto the piazza. The large windows enable a flow of light and visibility between spaces. The piazza is not only a social space but an aesthetic space, filled with many beautiful things – a flower submerged in a glass vase, a candle floating in a bowl of water, a bowl of fruit, a print on the wall by Monet. This is a space in which the children take special care of each other and of what is around them.

Trollet had, at the time of my early visits, an outstanding cook who provided breakfast, lunch, and morning and afternoon tea. When lunch was served the children competently served themselves from each hot dish and at the table poured out their own glasses of water. They sat around the dining table with their teachers, chatting quietly to each other across the table, and passing bowls of salad to each other, using knives and forks competently – constituting the group as a community of people who recognize each other, and who could draw me, an aging, English-speaking professor, into their community.

I begin with a story from my first day at Trollet:

As the five-year-old children sit in their home classroom listening to the teacher, I notice the physical connectedness of skin on skin, hand on hair, an extension of each into the collective. They know who they are, each in their specificity within specific one-on-one relations, but they also work together as a whole. As they sit around in a semi-circle on the tiered benches quietly attending to what the teacher is saying, they also attend to their relations with each other. A girl sits down on the lower tier, her bottom on the feet of a boy sitting on the higher tier. She wriggles a little, with a fleeting look of irritation on her face. The benches are not deep enough to accommodate both feet and bottoms. The boy shifts his legs to make room for the girl, so that his knees embrace her. She settles down comfortably, and he gently runs his fingers through her hair as they listen to the teacher. Both looked completely present in the moment, with each other, within the group. Two other boys sit close together, the foot of one stroking the foot of the other, two feet intertwined, gently, affectionately, without disrupting the flow of the lesson. As well, the children include me in the lesson by using words in English, and by seeking out eye contact with me.

At the end of this first group session, instead of going off to his allocated group activity, one boy decides to show me his favourite picture book. We sit together in animated discussion over his favourite picture, discussing its intricacies, he in Swedish and me in English. It is an exciting picture, with a bank in the middle and a tunnel under the bank through which robbers are crawling. One robber has already successfully robbed the bank and is running away. There are cowboys and Indians on horses fighting, and a cowboy buying an ice cream at an ice cream parlour. There are dogs barking and exotic mountains in the distance. There is much here for us to discuss. He tells a teacher, who briefly comes into the room to check that we are OK, that he finds it really exciting to talk to me – and indeed he is visibly excited, sometimes clutching his genitals in an ecstasy of delight – a *haecceity* found in the just-thisness of the emergent moment in which we are completely absorbed in the picture, in the book, and in our communication with each other. The teacher later tells me that she had been surprised at his visible and voluble animation, since he is a boy who rarely speaks.

After we finish with the book, he takes me by the hand and shows me around the whole preschool explaining who is in each of the areas that we can see through the windows, and he shows me what each space is for within the piazza. Although he speaks in Swedish, he also uses gestures and facial expressions that make his meanings clear to me.

The boy who does not usually speak initiates an encounter, here, in which he and I, together with a book, move outside the orderly striations of the teacher's plans for the day. In his openness to my difference he is able to create a space in which he can speak with animation and with joy. Together we sit down to explore the intricacies of a picture he loves. He draws my attention to particular details, looking at my face to see if I am attending, then telling me more, laughing as he does so. He draws me into his world and the world of the book. Because I can't speak Swedish, I can't obey any impulse I might have to re-territorialize the space with teacherly striations in which I direct and he follows. Like the boy I also discover new possibilities. I find myself listening to the sound of his voice, reading his body language and his facial expressions, opening myself up to his idea, his pleasure. His happiness spills over and becomes my happiness too, so that I experience that crossing over where "becoming and multiplicity are the same thing" (Deleuze and Guattari, 1987: 249). Our difference from each other, in particular our language difference, far from being a problem, was an asset in opening us up to what we could each become in relation to the other.

In drawing attention to these micro-moments of being, I am working against the grain of taken-for-granted ways of seeing (or not seeing) what it is that children can do. Through listening to children I want to make visible, within the everyday, the extraordinary capacities children have, and the emergent, the creative, the intra-active encounters they engage in as they do the ongoing work of bringing themselves and their community into being.

In this first encounter we have a space made up of two people and a book, not tracing habitual striations laid down elsewhere, but actively mapping a new possibility, each open to the other, to the affective flow between them. We are able to take this line of flight together, in part because of our openness to the unexpected, and in part because of the orderly plane of existence established by everyone else that makes the unexpected possible, permissible. The teacher checks that we are ok, and accepts that we have gone off into another order, other than the one she was establishing. She does not need to pull the boy back into her plan for the day; she is open to the experimental encounter in which the boy finds his words spilling out in a joyful torrent. Not only does the boy share his favourite picture, but he also discovers in himself a competent and voluble knowledge of how the different spaces of the preschool articulate with each other, and how he might share that knowledge with a stranger. In entering into this joyful encounter, in which, together, we form a powerful whole that is more than each of us had previously been, I discover the joy of letting go of my adult, teacherly self who presumes to already know and to know better, instead, learning how to listen with all my senses, and so, in intra-action with the boy and the book, to experience a moment of *haecceity* or grace. We were, in Rinaldi's sense, open to the universe where "there are no limits" (Rinaldi, 2006: 185).

The children's openness to experimental encounters, to becoming in new ways in relation to difference, was also evident in other ways that they responded to me, a stranger in their midst. While some were shy in the face of my lack of Swedish, others invented ways to engage with me, mobilizing multiple languages. Over lunch one day, I shared a table with the five-year-olds and with Birgitta Kennedy, the *pedagogista*,[1] who actively facilitated our conversation:

> A five-year-old boy who sat next to me at lunch was chatting away to me very intently, looking into my eyes as he spoke. I was puzzled that Birgitta didn't offer a translation for something so apparently important. I asked her to translate for us. She came round to our side of the lunch table and squatted down beside him, asking him to tell her what he was saying. When he hesitated, she asked him to whisper it into her ear. But still she couldn't understand him, and asked him to tell her in Swedish. He blushed and said he couldn't tell her, as he didn't know what he was saying since he did not yet understand English. Realizing, then, that I did not have to understand the meaning of the words, but to engage in conversation with him, to connect with him, I happily listened to him with all my senses. He stroked my bare arm as we talked and when I turned to talk to someone else, he planted a small sweet kiss on my arm.
>
> When I visited some of the children two years later, at their big school, this boy rushed up to meet me, and the affective surge of joy between us was there still. He clearly had not forgotten me, though he did not remember that he had talked to me in "English". "I must have been very clever when I was young," he said, when I reminded him of that earlier encounter.

In that earlier meeting the boy initiated an encounter in which our two bodies became an interconnected communicative part of the larger group at the lunch table. In this moment there were again two people, this time surrounded by others who joined together as a lunch-time community, and engaged in conversation across language boundaries, depending for the most part on Birgitta's attentive and detailed translations. One boy extended his communicative capacity and found a way to talk to me without the aid of translation. In doing so he made my heart melt, and he bound us together in a mutual entanglement of becoming with each other, and with those others who made up the community around the table – not forgetting the cook who had provided a meal so delicious that the children went back for second and third helpings. His openness to my difference extended my sensory awareness, my openness to difference and to unexpected connections and lines of flight.

The children thus drew me into their community, and connected me to it. No-one bid these children, as far as I know, to make me part of their world. I was potentially someone to be ignored with my lack of Swedish. But they worked to bring me into their community, and into the universe of possibilities that might be created in each new moment. They demonstrated their capacity to "'listen' to life in all its facets [and to] listen to others with generosity" (Rinaldi, 2006: 116). They taught me in doing so how I too could extend my capacity for listening and for becoming.

During my visits to Trollet, when I was not talking to the children or the teachers, I stood or sat quietly observing, and writing whatever I saw in my notebook. The children were curious about what I was writing, and often asked me what I was doing. Sometimes the answer that I was writing was enough, though occasionally the questions persisted until they grasped I was a kind of scientist, who was interested in what happens in preschools. Sometimes the children came close and watched me writing and asked could they write too, as happened one peaceful afternoon as the warm sun shone down on the playground.

I sit alone in the warm afternoon sun and a girl approaches me. She asks to write in my book so I give her my pencil and she does some careful small squiggles of writing. We have a lively, funny time passing the pencil back and forth. Her small writing grows larger and I introduce the possibility of drawing a picture together. As we pass the pencil back and forth I tell her some English words connected to what we are drawing and she grows very confident with repeating them. Shoes, pink shoes, heart, hair, nose, lips, etc. Her drawing grows more and more confident as we go. I trace her hand and draw in the fingernails, which she "paints". I show her how to use the rubber on the end of the pencil to tidy the "nail-polish" up a bit. We put a poking out tongue on the mouth of the face we draw and she has fun poking out her own tongue then saying the name of it. Then her big sister comes to pick her up. She is happy to see her and makes no fuss about going.

Next day she comes to talk to me again. I talk to her in English and she shows by her facial expression that she doesn't understand. I comment that she has her pink shoes on. She beams and points to her pink t-shirt and to the rabbit on it. I comment that her t-shirt is pink and has a rabbit on it and she nods happily. Is this enough? No. She wants me to watch her on the ropes. She wants me to see how strong she is. I praise her for her strength and she looks very happy. She has again successfully initiated a positive flow of affect between us. She picks up a stick and "draws" on my page. She brings two buckets and a spade and persuades me to fill one of the buckets with sand. Briefly this turns into planting sticks and leaves in plant pots. Soon after she pulls the sticks and leaves out of the sand. She persuades me to take turns with the spade, putting more sand into the buckets. She tells me she is getting some water. *Vatten.* She pours the water into the two buckets and they overflow. She plays with the overflowing water, satisfied, and when it all soaks away into the sand she goes off to get more water. She is content that I am standing here writing. She brings another bucket of water and pours it in. It overflows and she builds a dam, then walks in the dam, stamping in the water. She joyfully kicks the sand then smoothes out the wet sand. I have a moment of anxiety about the beautiful pink shoes becoming wet and dirty but manage to let it pass. How easy it would have been for me to spoil this moment of happiness! My lack of Swedish again puts a useful trip on my tongue. This sequence is repeated, faster, until the water disappears. Now the buckets are full of soup to eat. The prac teacher joins us. She has one of those instant moments of anxious protest when the water flows everywhere and the buckets of sand become soup, "No!" she says, as if it is all becoming too chaotic, but she lets it go and "tastes" the soup. The girl is delighted that the teacher goes along with the fact that the buckets now contain soup. Then the buckets are upturned to make castles. The castles are admired and then demolished by the girl jumping joyfully on them. Each transformation, pot plant to dam to smooth surface to soup to castle is joyful. The action (making the castle) is focused and concentrated, but the transformation from one thing to another is what is thrilling.

I am fascinated by the way I am affectively drawn into these encounters, and by the way my teacherly self has an impulse to intrude with unnecessary striations – those all-too-familiar institutionalized and authorized ways of knowing and being. I learn to see just how unnecessary my impulse to order is, precisely because of my lack of Swedish. Instead of saying "be careful" and dampening the experimental play down, I enter into the sensory pleasure of it. The child's quiet concentration, her calm, spills over into my body, and I relax and enjoy the light of the afternoon sun on the leaves, the warmth of it on my back, the fresh chill on the air and the child quietly playing in the sand. I learn to enjoy the exciting transformations instead of worrying. Excitement spills from one to the other. And I see too how excitement can, in a split second, turn to anxiety and a wish for the experimentation to stop.

I saw that vividly this same morning between two children on the swings. They are close friends and love to swing together on the same swing, but she likes to swing high and he does not. When the swing went too high there were eventually tears on both sides. Excitement, and then a fear of danger. A step too far and the excitement lurches into fear and a reversion to the safety of old patterns and striations. The line of descent re-asserts itself.

I am fascinated, as I watch the children play, by the way affect is a quality of a collective rather than an individual. On this particular morning I see that courage too is an affect that can spill from one to another:

Three children are trying to scale a huge granite rock. One boy succeeds and he sits on the top and beams encouragement at the ones still trying to reach the top. His body experiences the surge of the others' determination, and so does mine as I watch. The girl is so tiny, but she wills her muscles to be strong, and the boys behind her and before her share in her courage and look happy. But suddenly she falls. The boys' bodies immediately switch to alarm, shouting to the teacher who comes running. Courage swings swiftly to alarm. Is she OK? Does she want to leave the big rock? But no, her affect swings back to courage. The rock is so much bigger than she is, but she tries again, and courage flows between the three. In a way it doesn't matter if she succeeds. It is the courageous leap, the momentary clinging on, and then the slide down the rock face, followed by circling round for another turn, after standing and watching the boy have his turn. But then a bigger boy runs up and goes straight up the rock face and takes up almost all the space on the top. The small boy leaps and makes it too. There are now three boys on the top and they are not making any room for the girl. The courage that flowed among the original three is gone, and the girl turns quietly and leaves.

For the time the two small boys and the even-smaller girl worked together to scale the rock, they combined to form a powerful whole. Their courage and determination to accomplish what seemed impossible passed affectively between them, and it spread to me as I watched. The courage of the one who successfully climbed the rock became the courage of the other two. The not-yet-known – how to climb the rock – was something each was determined to discover despite the temporary set-back when the girl fell. When the larger boy joined in, showing how it is done, the second boy suddenly acquired the bodily knowledge he had been striving for, and scaled the rock. But there was no space left on the top of the rock, and no affective courage flowing to the small girl. The original threesome was decomposed. The girl lost the bodily cohesion that she had had when part of the alliance with the two boys. The rock became a boys' rock, and the possibility of scaling it belonged, for the moment, to the three newly allied boys.

As alliances shift, so power transfers from one group to another. If the boys' allied power in taking over the space were to become cemented as both good and necessary (only boys should climb rocks), then the community would have a problem to solve – decompositions to engage in.

I am not separate from any of these observations. Even when I stand on the borders and observe, the affective flow of what I see engages me materially, conceptually, and ethically. I am not a pre-existing entity who sees something that exists independent of my gaze, but inextricably part of it all, constantly becoming, just as the children are intra-actively becoming within the emergent community we are collectively producing. My personal history with gender means I am alert to the possibility of gendered lines becoming fixed in oppressive striations. The intra-action on the rock alerts me to that possibility but it does not become evident as a repeated pattern.

(In)conclusion

Each encounter with a child brings us to a threshold, and to a new pact. The boy with the book and the boy at lunch opened up for me the possibility of listening without knowing the meaning of the words, and of entering into a relational heterogeneous community-in-the-making; they taught me to be aware of affect and of the movement in-between one and another where each is open to being affected by the other. They opened up moments of *haecceity* or grace, so that I was no longer the person I had been before. In experiencing that affective flow I became more attuned to it in others – such as the children playing together scaling the rock face, or the children on the swing. To be immersed in this community was to be constantly crossing thresholds, entering new doors, learning new languages – as I did with the girl who began to draw and write with me and to speak some of my language, who later drew me into eating "soup" with her in the sandpit and into taking pleasure in each transformative line of flight, when everything changed in a joyful rush.

To enter into joyful compositions with the children we encounter, is to "combine to form a more powerful whole" (Deleuze, 1988: 19), a whole that enables us to compose ourselves anew, and for the children we encounter to compose themselves anew, such that each experiences an increase in joy, as well as, crucially, an increase in the power to think and to act. Such encounters open each particular being to the intensity of their own experience in relation to others.

In order to listen to children in a way that respects and enables the contribution to their communities that they might make, one must be open to being affected. Encounters with others, where each is open to being affected by the other, are integral, I have argued, to the life of the community itself. Our capacity to affect each other, to enter into composition with others both enhances our specificity and expands our capacity for thought and for action. It is that openness to entering into composition with heterogeneous others in an ongoing way that enables a community to become and to evolve, through all its coexisting multiplicity. Its emergence as an ethical place depends not just on striations laid down by powerful forces, but on openness to emergent difference in the other and in oneself, and openness to the not-yet-known, with all the riskiness that that might entail.

In the next chapter I reflect on two kinds of listening – emergent listening, and listening-as-usual. These thoughts on listening are diffracted with stories from the community I live in, stories from preschools in Jönköping and also from Trollet, and finally from Virginia Woolf's memoirs.

Note

1 A *pedagogista* works with the pedagogues/teachers to lead their development and further education through projects and staff group workshops and meetings.

Chapter 2

Emergent listening as creative evolution

[I]t might be said of life, as of consciousness, that at every moment it is creating something.

(Bergson, 1998: 29)

In Chapter 1 I explored the way in which the two lines of force, ascent and descent, depend on each other. Regularity and repetition, the line of descent, holds things the same, while creative lines of flight that open up new modes of thought and ways of being, or lines of ascent, are at one and the same time necessary for life, sometimes dangerous, and always subject to being re-incorporated back into lines of descent. In this chapter I will extend my analysis of the concept and practice of listening in terms of these two lines of force.

What we usually think of as listening, particularly as adults listening to children, is most closely aligned with lines of descent; we listen in order to fit what we hear into what we already know. The Reggio Emilia approach to listening, what I will call here emergent listening, is more closely aligned with the line of ascent. The tension between these two interdependent modes is integral to what Bergson calls creative evolution, *which depends both on the existence of, and the capacity to let go of, the status quo.*

Emergent listening is not a simple extension of usual practices of listening. It involves working, to some extent, against oneself, and against those habitual practices through which one establishes "this is who I am". It presents a major challenge to liberal humanist and phenomenological constructs of what it means to be human, where those constructs begin with the concept of self as an entity that is continually judged against an imagined ideal, and found wanting (Davies, 2010).

Emergent listening "requires a suspension of our judgements and above all our prejudices" (Rinaldi, 2006: 65). But more than this, it means opening up the ongoing possibility of coming to see life, and one's relation to it, in new and surprising ways. Emergent listening might begin with what is known, but it is open to creatively evolving into something new. Emergent listening opens up the possibility of new ways of knowing and new ways of being, both for those who listen and those who are listened to. As Rinaldi (2006: 114) says: "Learning how to listen is a difficult undertaking; you have to open yourself to others . . . Competent listening creates a deep opening and predisposition toward change". That predisposition toward change, I will suggest, is a vital element of creative evolution (Bergson, 1998).

My first story in this chapter comes from my own community, a 1920s inner-city apartment block in a quiet, leafy street adjacent to the popular tourist nightclub destination of Kings Cross (Davies, 2009a). The people who live in my street include professors, like me, architects, actors, business-men and -women, teachers, young families with small children, ageing pensioners in their eighties – a richly diverse community, whose central hub is the coffee shop, next door to my apartment block.

One morning, when I was sitting in the coffee shop reading, Claudia, who lives in my apartment block, brought Clementine in, asking me to mind her for a while. Clementine was around eight months old at the time, and I was more than happy to help out. Later I wrote:

> I was sitting on a bench and leaning back against the wall. Clementine was climbing on the pile of pillows on the bench beside me. Suddenly she jerked forward and her head banged hard against the wall. She pulled back, surprised. I waited, listening with all my senses, open to whatever she might need from me. She was quite still, and quiet, and I figured the "accident" was over. Then she leaned forward slowly, carefully, and bumped her head softly against the wall, and drew back. She repeated this movement several times with different levels of speed – none of them fast enough to cause a painful repeat of the first encounter.

Each careful movement, forward and back, generated a new embodied knowledge of self-in-motion, self-intra-acting with the matter that made up the place where we were sitting. The repeated, experimental movement risked a repeat of the initial painful bump, but in creatively and thoughtfully entering the space of the accident, crossing and re-crossing its threshold, she generated knowledge about her body, and new bodily skill, in relation to the wall, that might enable her to prevent any future accidental collisions.

There are two threads of this story that interest me. One is the creative exploration that Clementine engaged in, revealing her willing vulnerability in the face of the not-yet-known. The other is my own intense pleasure in becoming aware of the creative life force that her experiment made visible.

In this moment of being with Clementine I found myself listening to her in a way that enabled me to see how she explored the relation between her body and the space around her. I did not immediately move her away from the wall, not because I knew what would happen next, and certainly not because I planned what happened next. What happened took me by surprise, and I found myself responding to her with respect and with wonder – at her, but also at what she allowed me to glimpse – the creative desire to explore that is inherent in all life. It was a moment of grace in which I discovered a kinship with her, not based on similar identities, or shared genes, but a shared commitment to life's mobility. Who I was in that moment changed, and I found myself loving her without preconceptions.

Emergent listening as transgressive

Knowledge of the status quo is much valued in life generally. It gives one a kind of common sense (Kumashiro, 2008). It is often said of children that they need an orderly environment in which the boundaries are made clear. Knowledge of the status quo is productive, however, only as long as it does not become an investment in the status quo itself. Common sense can be a trap – presenting a series of lines of descent – that closes down creativity. Common sense is a powerful tool that can be used to shore up the status quo, or, alternatively, it can be used to find its cracks and crevices, its potential for change. Knowing how things work can allow you to change them, to know when rules can or should be broken, and to work out how to invent and create in ways that go beyond the already known. The cliché *children like to know the boundaries* is a dangerous half-truth. They like to know the boundaries, not only to create a safe and predictable space in which they know how to be competent, but also because they like to know how to successfully transgress those boundaries. In this sense emergent listening is transgressive.

Integral to listening to children is *being there* with the children and, as Schulte observes, that being there can involve getting lost:

> Lost, because being there through research is in part a practice of stray-ing afield; to take pleasure in one's digressions, to leave one's fixities through the curiosities of an astute inattention, and to harbor a love for what is unexpected and yes, unnerving. Being there with children through research is exactly that, a process of being there *with* children, a process of relations – a process of joyful yet unsettling reciprocity that is undeniably temporal and forever incomplete.
>
> (2013: 4)

The status quo, inside which identities and existing knowledges are lodged, gives way, in *being there* with the child, to a relational, emergent reality. That reality is not "objective", but "subjective", and that subjectivity is relational, multiple, and alive. It opens up inside moments of being, such as the moment with Clementine, where her exploratory strategy opened up for me an intra-active becoming, a line of ascent. We were both fully absorbed in the moment, and transformed in that moment.

Such moments of being are not produced through the unthinking repeti-tion of our *quotidian* lives – that is, our ordinary, everyday, common-place lives – but through moments of being in which something new and surprising opens up in-between one and another, in which each listens and comes to know differently, becoming different from the one they were before (Nancy, 2007). This is what Deleuze (1990) calls *haecceity* or grace.

Emergent listening has this double movement: one thinks differently and one becomes no longer the self one was before. What was there but invisible in the prior situation, that is, its *void*, becomes visible. The child jerking forward in an apparently random way, apparently not yet in control of her bodily movements, becomes the child who is developing an exquisite control of her body, who willingly takes risks, who experiments, and who rapidly acquires new knowledge and new relations between herself and others, where those others are not just the adult sitting beside her, but the bench, the cushions, and the wall (Bennett, 2010).

Taubman explores this difference between the status quo and openness to the void, drawing on the work of Badiou:

> There exists on the one hand the status quo, what Badiou calls the "state" of the situation, which consists of our quotidian lives – dogmatic opinions, institutionalized knowledges, habits, bureaucratic allegiances, and the pursuit of fulfilling our animal appetites. It is, if you will, the conditioned life, the doxa, or, in psychoanalytic terms, the un-examined, overdetermined life. . . . On the other hand there is what Badiou calls "subjective truth", which only emerges when a situation suddenly, as if by chance, or what Badiou will call grace, shifts, revealing what had, until that moment, been a void in the situation. This shift reveals what had always been there but had remained invisible, until a subject commits to the consequences of the event, allowing that event to unfold as the truth of the situation.
>
> (Taubman, 2010: 198–199)

We might describe the status quo in this story of Clementine as the risk-averse society in which vulnerable children are protected from misadventure. The void, or that which is not visible within that status quo, is, in this moment of being, the ongoing engagement of living beings, even very small children, in creative evolution, and the experimental acquisition of new self–other relations. In the pause after the first bump, a pause in which I did not know what to expect, I experienced a moment in which new knowledge and new ways of being and knowing became possible, not only for the child but also for me in my capacity as one who listened to the child, open to what might emerge in that moment.

But this openness to the new is difficult to hold on to. Emergent listening is always in tension with a tendency to make things solid, to classify them, to territorialize them. We continually attempt to fix the unfixable in place. We incorporate the new and unexpected movement into the already known, we regulate it in the hope of holding and repeating it. But you can't plan such experimental moments of head-banging. Nor can you regulate adults to notice them when they do occur. The desire to regulate and control, exacerbated these days by neoliberal governments (Davies and Bansel, 2007a, b), creates an ever-present danger of turning emergent listening, and the related strategies of attention, into listening-as-usual, that is, into, repetitive listening, not requiring any thought, and serving to reiterate that which is already known.

Documentation: A listening strategy

Documentation is a primary strategy in Reggio-Emilia-inspired schools through which the new is made visible and opened up for thought and extension. Children's thoughts and the images they have created are put up on the walls so anyone passing by can contemplate the emergent multiplicity of the life of the preschool. Ceppi and Zini, Reggio-Emilia-inspired architects, draw attention to the materiality of the preschool space and to its creative force: "The environment generates a sort of psychic skin, an energy giving second skin made of writings, images, materials, objects, and colors, which reveals the presence of the children even in their absence" (Ceppi and Zini, 1998: 17).

The double movement of ascent and descent, opening up to the new, and re-establishing the state of the situation, emerged in discussions with Karin Alnervik, Director of HallonEtt in Jönköping. Karin is interested in exploring the idea that documentation is not always innocent. While documentation plays a central role in the Reggio process of listening and opening up for new thought, it can also become so incorporated into the quotidian practices, the striations, of institutional life-as-usual that it serves no more than the reproduction of that institutional life. It may even take on a life of its own that forecloses listening. The technology of documentation can serve to shape the very thing that it sets out to document, rather than facilitating the emergence of the not-yet-known.

Karin's own practices of documentation actively work towards keeping the documentation open and alive. The children's words and images are put on the walls in a way that makes it clear that they are work in progress – rather than finished works of art. She finds that some of the teachers in her preschools struggle with this. They prefer displays that are more orderly, more clearly accomplished as works of art, and that are beautifully displayed. But in order to keep the walls alive, to make a commitment to life as mobility itself, in which the not-yet-known of the children's thoughts has space to emerge, the photos and paintings, along with quotes from what the children say, are posted on the wall in an informal way that invites the passer-by, both child and adult, to stop and contemplate what it is that is emergent there. It invites them to be affected by it, and to wonder how they might become involved in it, how they might add to it or respond to it. Such informal displays invite not only additions and extensions, but shifts of consciousness that open up thought in those who view them. Karin's walls thus actively *invite* emergent intra-actions. They *invite* further thought. They *tell* a story of thinking something through. The walls, too, like life, can be mobile, creative (Ceppi and Zini, 1998).

A story Karin told me of a wall being alive illustrates this point of Ceppi and Zini's beautifully:

> On this particular day the teacher had written a child's story on an over-head transparency. The child shone her story up on to the wall. In the space between the projector and the wall, the child turned round and round, exploring the play of light and words on her skin, on her dress. The words were like mist or rain that she could walk through, she said. They surrounded her and went through her. Her story was not just on the wall, but in the air, on her body, going through her body. She put a block of wood on the wall over particular words, so the word shone onto the wood. "Is this word my name?" she asked.

In this story a magical and unexpected moment is opened up, where the status quo gives way to a new way of experiencing words, of intra-acting with writing, of the child making the words her own in entirely new ways. These emergent moments of grace, or *haecceity*, are vital to movement, and to dissolving old fixities. *Haecceity*, or just-this-ness, is integral to what Deleuze calls de-territorialized, smooth space – the space that escapes over-coded striations. Smooth space enables an immersion in the present moment, in time and in space, that often eludes us in the press of normative expectations, of habitually repeated thoughts, and practices and structures.

> A haecceity is a moment of pure speed and intensity (an individuation) – like when a swimming body becomes-wave and is momentarily suspended in nothing but an intensity of forces and rhythms. Or like when body becomes-horizon such that it feels only the interplay between curves and surfaces and knows nothing of here and there, observer and observed.
>
> (Halsey, 2007: 146)

Or when words and light and body merge in a joyful, exploratory dance, where written words are no longer separate and alien, but intimate and familiar.

Documentation can be an ephemeral but vital means of opening up new ways of thinking and being, keeping thought in motion and opening children and teachers up to a line of ascent. But the line of descent is still always at play, re-incorporating the children's work back into the striations of the status quo. The children's words and artwork can become, for example, exploitable products to be used as material for books that are marketable, or they can be transformed into "evidence" of the school's good teaching, or of a particular teacher's excellence. Lines of descent have the potential to close down emergent listening. Such closing down, in all probability, will not take place at a conscious level; it almost certainly will not be intentional. The production of exploitable materials may be understood, by those managing their production, as no more than a rational means of acquiring necessary funds, or building a school's or a teacher's profile. But giving productivity primacy can lead to an incalculable loss of *haecceity*, of being emergent in the moment, of the creative evolution of thought and being. That loss you could call the void in the production of marketable or assessable products.

My next story about documentation emerged in a discussion with teachers in Jönköping about a series of photos one had taken to document the children's sense of place, which was the collective Reggio Emilia research theme that particular year.

> The children are exploring parkland near their school. They hear some birds and although they look, they cannot find them. The teacher asks: "What else can you find?" The next photo in the teacher's documentation shows a child's finger pointing at a clover flower.

Putting to one side the dominance of visual documentation that has taken over from the auditory, the interesting question that is opened up here is who is the agent in this scene of the finger pointing? Is the camera recording a spontaneous moment of wonder, where the child notices the flower, and perhaps sees vividly for the first time the pale pink sphere made up of many small trumpet-shaped flowers. In such a scenario you might say the child is the agent, caught up in a moment of grace, of *haecceity*.

Or is the teacher the agent, deciding they are not looking for birds, but for something else that can be visually documented with the camera. Or more controversially, is the camera the agent? Are teachers and children together caught up in a quest ruled by what is photographable by this specific camera? The camera, being digital, and having a zoom lens, can capture the flower and the finger pointing. Moreover, the digital technology has made children much more conscious of what the camera can do, and how activity can be organized to meet its demands. Or, yet another reading might lead us to ask: is the technology of documentation itself the agent?

What might the teacher and the children be doing if the time spent in the park were not responding to the technology of documentation? Might they have sat quietly and listened to the bird-song? Might they have picked the flower and smelled it? Might they have decided to investigate the structure of the flower rather than being content with the photo? Or might they simply have run and jumped and shouted, exploring sound and spatiality – air in lungs, grass on skin, bodies moving through space, tumbling together on grass, opening up other possibilities of being in the park?

It is easy to romanticize such an image, and to see the documentation as intrusive, even controlling. It is important to re-emphasize, therefore, the vital role that documentation can play in opening up creative movement toward the not-yet-known, and in interrupting the quotidian practices through which life-as-usual is maintained. This photographic moment of finger-pointing may well have been such a moment.

Documentation invites participants in any moment of being to be aware of being, and to be open to thought and its emergent multiplicities. Objects like walls and cameras are intra-active players in these scenes, and it is important to be aware of our relationship with them. Not just our physical relationship with them, but our psychic investments in them. We can use them to hold the status quo in place (just as walls and cameras hold prisoners in place), or, as Karin showed, as a means of opening up the joyful and unexpected – the line of flight beyond the already known.

The point that Bergson, and also Deleuze and Guattari, make is that lines of descent, and their striations, are always waiting to re-assert themselves. As adults working, and playing, with children, we may inadvertently import those striations and initiate those lines of descent through our own unexamined desires. Teachers are involved in making constant choices, and in making those choices it is vital, Taubman says, to be faithful "to the process of examining [one's] own libidinal investment in that choice" (Taubman, 2010: 210). Self-interest is "an over-determined attachment and a defence against change" (Taubman, 2010: 210). Furthermore, he suggests that, "Renouncing or waffling on the rigor of analysis constitutes a betrayal of ourselves, for we then become blind to our involvement in our reality, and risk succumbing to what Badiou labels the maxim of opinion which is: 'Love only that which you have always believed'" (Taubman, 2010: 211, citing Badiou, 2001: 52). We may, without realizing it, be resistant to encounters in which we are open to being affected, because of unexamined attachments to some aspect of the status quo.

Emergent listening is demanding. It means not confining oneself to opinion, or to what one has always believed or wanted. It involves the suspension of judgement, letting go of the status quo and of the quotidian lives embedded in that status quo. It opens one up for new ways of knowing and being, actively resisting closure and being curious about the void of any situation. And, finally, it requires a rigorous awareness of one's own desires and libidinal investments. Implicated in each of these is openness to one's own differentiation – to becoming different from oneself, but further, seeking ways of being no longer organized around the establishment and maintenance of self-interested identity.

Emergent listening as differentiation

Roffe describes the Deleuzian space of *differentiation*, or intra-active becoming, as first, "a moment of de-individualization, an escape to some degree from the limits of the individual" and second, "the constitution of new ways of being in the world, new ways of thinking and feeling, new ways of being a subject" (Roffe, 2007: 43). Differentiation does not fix subjects or objects in place, or tie them to static, individualistic, or binary identities – in which someone is always this *or* that, never *and*. It opens up a space where creative energies are mobilized through ongoing relations within the spaces that are generated. Differentiation is not based on a rejection of the already known, but on an assertion, rooted in philosophy, science, and art, that life generates and is generated through movement and invention; it both draws on the already known, and it generates something new (Davies, 2009b).

Differentiation is not unlike when the body first plunges into deep water. It must rapidly acquire new skills that are appropriate to the new space, while still carrying knowledge from the old. The new can be dangerous otherwise:

> He who throws himself into the water, having known only the resistance of the solid earth, will immediately be drowned if he does not struggle against the fluidity of the new environment: he must perforce still cling to that solidity, so to speak, which even water presents. Only on this condition can he get used to the fluid's fluidity. So of our thought, when it has decided to make the leap.
>
> (Bergson, 1998: 193)

In the following story from Trollet, Mirza, a three-year-old Bosnian boy without much Swedish, takes a plunge toward the new. Not unlike the body plunging into water for the first time, he discovers what the new medium of the sand in the sandbox might open up. Christina Nilsson, the *torgetpedagog*,[1] opens up the space in which this immersion of the self in the new medium can take place. My story begins when she is working with a small group made up of Mirza and two four-year-olds, Cora and Mats.

> After morning fruit time with Christina they begin constructing roads and buildings with the wooden blocks. After a while Mirza shifts his attention to the sandbox, which is nearby. In the middle of it is an inviting symmetrical pile of round balls made out of wet sand. He glances at Christina and then at me, waiting for the word that says no. After a few seconds of hesitation he plunges his hand into the sand in one swift move. His bodily affect says he knows this is a risky move. Christina quietly tells him it is not time for the sandbox, and she shows him how to brush the sand off his hands, rubbing them together over the sandbox, which he does without any apparent resistance. But it is as if the sand is calling to him, and he turns back to the box, his body trembling, and plunges his hand back into the sand.
>
> Christina is meanwhile suggesting a new development with the road of blocks and another boy joins the building project. She quietly tells Mirza it is OK to play in the sand. Mirza gathers the balls of sand together with one scoop and squashes them together. He tries to make a new ball, but stops, not knowing how to do it. He runs his fingers through the sand while gazing into the distance, and then makes a small castle that he seems not to be satisfied with. He brushes the sand off his hands, as

Christina has shown him, and wanders off, brushing the last sand off on his trousers.

Cora comes to the sandpit and Mirza rejoins. Cora asks Christina to make new sand balls and she does so, showing them how to do it. This time the sandcastle is built high and patted down, with new shapes emerging, built up and then patted down. The two children continue working on their castle, talking quietly to each other. The words are like smooth water flowing between them.

It is time for all the children to go outside. Mirza tries to get the sand off his hands as instructed earlier, but they are still covered in sand. He rubs his hands on his trousers, then tries again to rub the sand off as Christina has shown him. He appeals to Christina and she tells him he can use water to wash it off. Cora joins in washing hands. Christina goes outside and Mimi is in charge of the square. Cora calls out loudly to Mimi to ask if they can stay inside during outside playtime. Mimi says yes. They return to the sandbox and Mirza reshapes the castle completely, making a separate peak from Cora's. He is happy now.

At first Christina called the children together for morning tea and then a project with the blocks. When Mirza strayed she gently called him back, redrawing his attention to the collaborative project with the blocks. She defined the space and time as block time and showed him how to extricate himself from the sandbox. But she also listened to him, to his body language, and she quickly saw how the sand pulled him back. At that moment other groups started to regroup with hers, and, going with the emergent possibilities, she let go of the specificity of the planned scenario of these particular children playing with blocks in this particular way. She quietly let Mirza know that it was OK if he played at the sandbox.

The movement between one kind of order and another emerged in response to the children's initiatives. Yet, despite his longing, Mirza found himself at a loss with the sand. When Cora joined him and began confidently building with sand, with him, Mirza watched and experimented in concert with her, and so discovered how to build with this new medium. As they played, Mirza and Cora were connected through eye contact and the sound of their voices, their body movements and facial expressions, mirroring each other in their mutual absorption in the wet sand. There was a connection through concerted action – playing with the sand – the rhythm of turns, the collaborative occupation of space, and of activity in space. They listened to each other, though their shared language was limited. Mirza's moment of trembling desire was thus transformed into a moment of grace, in which the children's selves-together-and-in-motion, in the medium of sand, unfolded.

The double movement of ascent and descent requires of us a willingness to give up on the status quo, and at the same time it requires faithfulness to desire, to being aware of desire, including the desire for safety and predictability, and its impact on the situation. It involves a commitment to the truth of oneself and the situation and, at the same time, being open to new truths, which may be in tension with the desire for stasis – for being an entity rather than an intra-active becoming.

My final story, taken from Virginia Woolf's *Moments of Being*, reveals the complexity of this double movement and the ever-present tendency to turn movement into stasis, ascent into descent:

> I was fighting with Thoby on the lawn. We were pommelling each other with our fists. Just as I raised my fist to hit him, I felt: why hurt another person? I dropped my hand instantly, and stood there, and let him beat me. I remember the feeling. It was a feeling of hopeless sadness. It was as if I became aware of something terrible; and of my own powerlessness. I slunk off alone, feeling horribly depressed . . . I was quite unable to deal with the pain of discovering that people hurt each other.
>
> (Woolf, 1978: 82–83)

At the beginning the story tells of a descent, one might say, into a predictable childhood fight. The fight, in Bergson's (1998) terms, can be seen as a line of descent, an automatic repetition not requiring any thought. But then the automatic unwinding of this particular fight is interrupted by a question, a question that opens a line of ascent into a new way of being perhaps; or a moment of insight that leads to something new. But no, the child is horribly depressed. She feels utterly powerless. She has descended into something far worse than the fight – a willing acceptance of her own powerlessness. Is the question *"why hurt another person?"* not only the discovery of an important guiding principle that can be weighed and balanced against other principles, but also a line of descent, this time a gendered one?

A new thought can rapidly become stifling if multiplicity and openness to emergence are abandoned. As Bergson expresses it:

> Our freedom, in the very movements by which it is affirmed, creates the growing habits that will stifle it if it fails to renew itself by a constant effort: it is dogged by automatism. The most living thought becomes frigid in the formula that expresses it. The word turns against the idea.
>
> (Bergson, 1998: 127)

In the middle-class Victorian England of 1890, when Virginia was eight years old, the gendered status quo had no place for the spirited girl who believed she had a right to defend herself with force. At the same time, I would like to suggest that the void of this story, its invisible presence, is the de-territorializing of that utterly depressing status quo, which Virginia later conducted through her writing. The depth of despair that she felt in taking up that passive position as her own, remained with her into adulthood. She wrote about it and reflected on it in her memoirs, and it is present as an underlying question in all her fictional writing. The normalizing force of her question "*why hurt another person?*" had the power not only to stop her fighting, but also to allow herself to be beaten. That gendered line of descent would later come to be a driving force in the difficult ascent into the not-yet-known that runs through all of her writing. The vividness of the moment, its intensity, opens up the possibility that the moment will become much more than a simple replaying of the already known.

(In)conclusion

In this chapter I have talked about the inevitable struggle involved in listening as continual openness to the not-yet-known. Emergent listening is being open to being affected by the other, and to the possibility of moments of *haecceity* or grace, when everything changes. It opens up in the relational space in between emergent multiplicities, the possibility of community, and the creative evolution of life itself. Emergent listening is in tension with, and yet also depends on, the predictable patterns of life-as-usual, the repetitions and striations out of which difference might emerge. The technologies of listening can produce not the active unfolding of the new, and the mobility of life itself, but a form of closure or foreclosure. Bergson distinguishes these two movements of opening and closing as ascent and descent, which he sees as related, universal movements. Listening to children catches us up in the ordinary repetitions of everyday life, and it also opens up for them, and for us, those moments of *haecceity* or grace in which every moment is creating something. The small child's experimentation with her relationship with the wall, another's experiment with words as light shining on her body, and a third child's exploration of the properties of sand – each of these can affect those who listen to them. That listening may require of them a willingness to be lost, to relax their tight grip on the status quo, to enable them to be in the *haecceity* of the moment when everything changes. The lines of descent and ascent are constantly affecting each other and it is not possible to separate them. An apparent line of ascent – a new question like "why hurt another person?" – can plunge you into a binding, apparently fixed line of descent. And lines of ascent are sometimes risky and even dangerous.

I began this chapter with the words from Bergson: "it might be said of life, as of consciousness, that at every moment it is creating something" (1998: 29). To engage in emergent listening is to tap into that creative force in children and in oneself – an extraordinary gift to both.

In the next chapter I turn to the tension experienced between the self as identity and the self as emergent and multiple. These two possibilities of self, like the lines of ascent and descent, cannot actually be separated from each other, and, like the lines of ascent and descent, they depend on each other.

Note

1 Just as there is a teacher solely responsible for planning and supervising activities in the garden, so there is a *torgetpedagog*, a teacher whose task it is to organize activities in the central piazza or square, such as cooking, the creation of large communal artworks, or special celebratory events. Here children meet and play with children outside their usual groupings engaging in activities that Christina has planned for them. The *torgetpedagog* is literally the pedagogue of the square.

Chapter 3

Intra-active becoming

In Chapter 2 I made a distinction between emergent listening and the more usual taken-for-granted practices of listening. I explored the idea that these are not entirely separate ways of listening, but linked to lines of flight on one hand and striations on the other, which actually depend on each other. In this chapter I want to think about the nature of the ~~subject~~ who might listen or be listened to.[1] What I anticipate is an entangled intra-action between, on the one hand, listening-as-usual, where the subject who is listening or being listened to has a hearable, recognizable identity, and on the other hand, emergent listening, where the ~~subject~~ is not so much an entity as an intra-active becoming. As with lines of ascent and descent, I anticipate that these two kinds of subject cannot actually be separated, and that they too depend on each other.

Listening-as-usual produces individual selves who have an identity that can be grasped through already existing categories. Their characters are constantly judged, both by themselves and others, as at risk of falling short of the ideal of what human subjects ought to be. That fear of not being good enough is exacerbated under neoliberal regimes currently dominating most western governments and their state institutions. Neoliberalism heightens individualism by intensifying competition at school and at work, removing social safety nets, and making the management of risk an individual responsibility (Davies and Bansel, 2005, 2007a, b). Each individual's attempts to live up to the ideal are read in terms of free choice – anyone can succeed if they make the right choices. And the choices they make will be judged in moral terms, revealing, or not revealing, their good character (Deleuze, 1980).

I have elsewhere called this idea of the individualized self the subject-of-will (Davies, 2010), since its will is what is understood as informing its choices, and those choices in turn define its identity. This is the self who longs for recognition of itself, desiring that recognition as an affirmation of what it *really* is, a reality that is taken to exist prior to any act of recognition (Davies *et al.*, 2013). This self who *has* an identity is identified with ego, and is caught up in the defence of itself against the other – the other who will judge it and find it wanting, and who will in turn be judged.

With the aid of poststructuralist concepts, such as those being mobilized here in this book, this conception of the subject has been put under erasure. The intra-actively becoming ~~subject~~ is re-conceptualized as an emergent, relational being. Its difference from another is not a categorical difference, but a matter of becoming different or differentiation, not separate from other ~~subjects~~ but part of the same Being (Davies and Gannon, 2009). In this way of thinking, we are all made of the same matter, and inhabit the same humanity. This is not a simple either/or, however. We are neither the singular subjected being nor the collective terms of our subjection, but singular *and* plural, where singularity can refer to all of humanity, and plurality can refer to each one of us. Deleuze plays with this thought when he writes about the "single and same voice for the whole thousand-voiced multiple, a single and unique Ocean for all the drops, a single clamor of Being for all beings" (Deleuze, 1994: 304).

In order to grasp the difference between these differing conceptualizations – of the ~~subject~~ and the subject – it is important to understand that they are not equivalent, substitutable concepts, nor do they refer to discrete, substitutable ways of being and knowing.

The self-as-identity takes its meaning inside the binary singular/plural. "I" is singular and takes its definition against "society", which is plural. This individualized subject is understood as an active agent and the construction of it as such within western cultures is so pervasive that it is difficult to think against the grain of it, or to imagine that agency might indeed be blocked by this constitution of subjects as individualized identities. The ~~subject~~ as intra-active becoming, in contrast, is both singular *and* plural. Its plurality lies in itself, in its own multiple singularities, and in the multiplicity of beings who are co-implicated in Being.

The individualized subject's *specificity* is ontologically real; and it observably works to accomplish a sense of itself as coherent, knowable, continuous, and predictable – as an identity (Bergson, 1998). But that orderly predictability itself can be the foundation of its own limitations and its vulnerability to institutional coercion and control, its lack of agency.

Listening to the other, for the self-as-identity, is to judge against an imagined ideal and to find it wanting. Listening is, at the same time, used to define the borders of one's being – it establishes "This is what I am not", or, "This is the same as me – what I am". But lacking distance from its own listening it is also swept along by dominant ways of thinking and speaking, becoming what those modes of enunciation anticipate of it. Its own capacities for ethical thought and practice are limited by its primary attachment to the self–other binary, and to self's survival.

In contrast, listening to the other, for the ~~subject~~-as-intra-active-becoming, involves listening to thought happening, putting itself up against thought to see what might be unfolded with it. Listening is not just to oneself and the other, but to the intensities of forces working on us and through us. It listens to changing, emergent thought, and is co-implicated in it, diffracting with it.

It is in this capacity to listen to emergent thought and to the "thousand-voiced multiple" that its agency lies.

The individualized self-as-identity, then, is not, as it might have imagined, the beginning, or even the *end-point* of itself, but the potential sticking point, the place where thought can get stuck inside the already known. It has difficulty detaching itself from what it is, and from what it knows, since its identity is bound up with the production of already existing knowledge. And identity, for the self-as-identity, is all-important. There is a certain narcissism and paranoia in this subject. It positions itself and is positioned within the repeated citations of the already known, gazing upon itself as if it were original and unique, continually needing to defend itself in not matching up to its own idea of, and ideal for, itself.

The conceptual shift, from the self-as-identity to the subject-as-intra-active-becoming, is a shift away from will, intentionality, and repetition, toward *receptiveness* to the not-yet-known (of self and other), and toward emergent possibilities of thought and being where being includes all beings, human, animal, and earth. In being open to the possibilities that such thought opens up, one must struggle *against* the limitations of the individualized self-as-identity. To be and become that emergent subject requires constant work against the seductions of the lines of descent that require no effort, that confirm who one is and how the world works. To be an intra-actively emergent subject is not the result of a "spontaneous effusion of a personal capacity. It is the power, won only with the greatest difficulty *against oneself*, of being constrained to the world's play" (Badiou, 2000: 11). It is not enough to *decide* to be such a subject; one has to struggle against oneself, against the normative force of language and everyday practice. It is a continuous struggle. At the same time, to be recognizably someone, to have an identity, is necessary for survival. It provides a safe plot of land in which to rest from that struggle.

Deleuze and Guattari's (1987) concept of the "schizo" captures something of the subject intra-actively becoming, which they contrast with the self-as-identity or "paranoid man". As Colebrook (2002: 5) says, "Their [concept of] 'schizo' is not a psychological type (not a schizophrenic), but a way of thinking a life not governed by any fixed norm or image of self – a self in flux and becoming, rather than a self that has submitted to law".

The struggle against oneself as an individualized self-as-identity, involves stepping back from habitual ways of acting and reacting. Individualized selves are more used to struggling against each other, and positioning themselves inside those citational chains through which they have made sense of themselves, all the while understanding themselves, paradoxically, as original, and as painfully unable to live out, perfectly, their own ideal image (Davies and Harré, 1990; Davies, 2008).

The subject-as-intra-active-becoming is not centre stage in its own life, and is not dependent on recognition within normative discourses. In the face of the not-yet-known, the subject-as-intra-active-becoming does not leap to normative or moralistic judgements, or to abjecting the other, but participates in the unfolding event, and in the evolutionary impulse to create new possibilities. It is here, I suggest, that agency lies, not in individual wilful acts, but in the creative evolution made possible through openness to the other and to the not-yet-known.

The subject-as-intra-active-becoming is not locked down inside the striations of the already known. It is an emergent facet of being, its senses and its imagination are open to the expressive modalities of being. Its being is ontologically connected to all Being. In poststructuralist thinking, creative evolution does not spring ready made out of the brow of the individual thinker; it arises out of emergent Being, out of listening to the multiplicities of being, out of being open to becoming a place where thought happens. Thought is an act, a movement, not separable from Being, and not possessed by one individual alone.

Children intra-actively becoming

I begin my diffractive entanglement of stories and concepts in this chapter with a story told in a collective biography workshop. Collective biography is a set of methodic practices in which memory and listening work together. The collective biography participants tell stories and listen to stories, and through their careful detailed listening and questioning, the storyteller is able to tell the story in detail, then write it and read it out loud to the assembled group. It is *collective* biography because in this process of listening and telling the stories lose their significance as stories of self-identity, and take on a quality of the thousand-voiced multiplicity of Being. This particular story is about listening. It involves the child, in Nancy's words, in stretching her ears: "an expression that evokes a singular mobility, among the sensory apparatuses, of the pinna of the ear – it is an intensification and a concern, a curiosity or an anxiety" (Nancy, 2007: 5):

> The teacher opened up a box of musical instruments. She asked who would like the tambourines, who would like the drums, and, last of all, who would like the triangles. The small girl had never played with any of these instruments, so she did not raise her hand. The triangles were given to the last ones left who had chosen no instruments. The triangles seemed inferior, the small girl thought, when compared to the drums. The teacher demonstrated how each instrument was to be played. The triangle must be held so, by the string, and struck just so with the small metal stick. Then the teacher sat down at the piano and played them the tune they were to accompany. Then again, with the children this time, and the noise was terrible, the children seeming to ignore completely the sound coming from the piano. The small girl carefully hit her triangle, but the sound was ugly and flat. The other triangle children ran their stick around the triangle hitting all the sides, laughing, making the triangle fly off in all directions with a jangling sound muddled up with the whack and thump of the drums and

the terrible jingling of the tambourines. She anxiously watched the other children's wild experimentation with their instruments until, suddenly, she could see that she must loosen her grasp on the stick before the triangle would sing. When the piano started again she noticed the sound of her triangle came after the note she was supposed to accompany. She listened hard, focused only on the piano, the triangle and the stick. The teacher repeated the tune. The small girl found she had to begin to strike not when the piano note came, but the moment before it came. Her body discovered exactly the moment the stick must begin its descent in order for the two sounds to come together. The sound of the piano and the triangle exactly together made a warm feeling in the small of her back that ran down the back of her legs and into her shoes.

In this moment the child listens for meaning, but much more than this, she listens for sound and the encounter among sounds. Her listening generates something new, a new knowing-being that enables her to play the triangle in concert with the piano. Her new-found knowledge seeps pleasurably through her body, changing her body's capacity to know, and to do, and to become. Her knowledge arises in the flows among multiple bodies – teacher-piano-striation, children-drums-triangles-tambourines, girl-triangle-stick, piano-triangle-teacher. In these diffractive encounters each flow affects the others (Barad, 2007; Davies and Gannon, 2013).

The girl's attentive listening is not just with ears for the teacher's meaning or intention. She listens with her whole body to the vibration of the piano and the timing of the beat, and she listens with all her senses to what the other children are able to produce in playing, wildly, with their instruments. Their wildness is not hers, but she learns nevertheless from their experimentation, though at first it repels her. In taking up her own experimentation she discovers a new way of moving in relation to others, discovering from her more playful, risk-taking peers that she needs to loosen her hold on the stick.

Together, the girl-stick-triangle open themselves to the experimentation of the other children, and become a new synchronicity in an encounter with the teacher-piano. The child has listened with all her being, and in an intra-active becoming finds herself co-creating an event that she could not have imagined beforehand, and that she could not have accomplished without her peers, the teacher, and the musical instruments. "To be listening is to be at the same time outside and inside, to be open from without and from within, hence from one to the other and from one in the other" (Nancy, 2007: 14). One listens to difference and is opened up into difference in an ongoing act of becoming – or differentiation.

The next two stories take us back to Trollet. I tell these stories in detail in order to invite you as reader into the moments of being that unfold there, asking you to listen, with me, to the children, to stretch your ears with me, to engage in a movement of "singular mobility" of the senses, "of the pinna of the ear" opening yourself to "intensification and a concern, a curiosity or an anxiety" (Nancy, 2007: 5).

> There are 12 four-year-olds assembled on the tiered wooden seats in the four-year-olds' room. The teacher sits facing them. The children are putting hands up for taking turns at speaking. Joshua comes in late with his mother, who gives the teacher two bananas in a plastic bag. The mother kneels down on the floor next to the teacher. She discusses the bananas with the teacher, explaining they are for morning tea since Joshua doesn't like the apples and pears that are provided in the preschool. The children sit quietly and listen and look. It is time for the mother to go. She kisses Joshua on the lips three times. He has his arms around her neck holding her tight. He lets her go, and turns towards the other children. Then he changes his mind and turns back flinging his arms around her for a fourth kiss. He finally lets her go, and his face falls into sadness. He sits down on the lower level of the seating, not close to any children in particular. His lower lip trembles and his head is bowed. The rest of the group is quiet, registering his sadness, enfolding him in quietness and sympathy, but leaving him alone, letting him gather himself together. There is no sign of rejection of this display of emotion or of his demonstration of longing for his mother.

This moment encapsulates the transition that every child makes every morning as they move from one relation to another, from being *this* ~~subject~~ in intra-action to *another* ~~subject~~ in intra-action. While it is often a visibly traumatic separation in the one-, two- and three-year-olds' transitions, needing help from the teachers or the other children to manage the transition, everyone assumes here that Joshua can manage the letting go of his embeddedness in one mode of being and his movement to another. Joshua intra-acting with his mother, and Joshua intra-acting with the others in this room are not separate. Joshua's mother negotiates difference for him with the teacher, while the other children listen. He is with his mother, who negotiates on his behalf. At the same time he is a member of the listening group of children, since he too is listening. When his mother leaves, he moves to become part of the group of children, becoming one of them but apart, as he struggles with the loss of himself-in-relation to his mother. The listening of the other children, in Nancy's terms, involves their openness to him, to being penetrated by his love and his struggle in letting go even while they sit silently listening.

The children do not abject Joshua by categorizing him as different, or by positioning him as needing to be turned into the same. They open themselves to the resonance of a mother who negotiates the possibility of bringing one's own fruit, speaking adult-to-adult on behalf of her son. They open themselves in their listening to the resonance of the kisses and the ambivalence of relinquishing the specificity of himself-in-relation to his mother. In that active listening, they create a space in which the movement goes from them as well as toward them, "from one to the other and from one in the other" (Nancy, 2007: 14). In this moment of being, the children, the mother, and the teacher create a context in which the specific ~~subject~~ known as Joshua becomes possible.

The context they performatively create is in part a repetition of previous such moments. It is a clear manifestation of the Swedish commitment to parental involvement in the life of preschools, and of the Reggio Emilia philosophy of difference as a value, and of empathy for the other. It is at the same time, emergent in the present moment, a moment in which Joshua's affect in relation to his mother can be fully experienced and expressed, and in which the listening children sense and acknowledge that affect with their silent listening and their non-judgemental gaze. The other children do not, as they might have done in another time or another place where individualism and normativity reign, mock him, or protest against the interruption to their "lesson". Joshua's preference for bananas and his emotional attachment to his mother, in the context of the children who listen, are performative. They establish not just that this is who Joshua is, but this is who *we* are (a "we" that includes Joshua): we are a group of people who encompass difference, and we are a group of people who know intensity of love and, equally, the expressed sorrow of parting. We each know ourselves and each other inside this moment that accomplishes who we are and who it is possible to be.

The children's knowledge of Joshua is not so much one that places him in a different category (the boy who comes late, the boy who doesn't like apples and pears, the boy who can't let his mother go, the boy who sits apart and shows his vulnerability), but a knowledge that it is OK to have food preferences, that mothers can be strong champions of their children, that love can be expressed openly and in public, that Joshua can be both one of them and yet separate and different. Each listening child, in Nancy's terms, is penetrated by that knowledge, each is opened to the possibility of knowing differently, to the safety of knowing differently, to expressing love openly, to taking risks. Each is open from without and from within to being different as they sit listening on the tiered wooden seats. No one moves to shame Joshua for being different; instead he is embraced by the careful listening of the others, even by those others whose own experiences may not have included such a loving and supportive mother. Joshua's love and his sorrow open up outside them and inside them, they become selves-in-relation to Joshua and each other, each becoming the self it is possible to be in this collective act of listening, not ontologically separate, but together realizing their being, even while each is recognizably a named and valued individuation within that being.

> Approximately 30 three-to-five-year-olds are assembled in the big square on the tiered wooden seats. They are singing together, facing Christina who leads the singing. She demonstrates the hand movements that go with this song. Joshua and his friend are in the back row. Joshua sings with his

mouth close to his friend's ear, facing his friend's ear rather than Christina. I'm not sure if he is singing the "correct" words of the song. The mischievous expression on his face suggests not. The friend into whose ear he is singing turns around and gives him a friendly hug – more like a cuddle, and then turns back to face the front, singing the song in synchrony with the teacher and the other children and carrying out the correct hand movements. Joshua, meanwhile, is inventing his own lines of flight making up different words and hand movements while still in synchrony with the teacher and the other children. His friend starts to follow his invented movements. They are now, at the same time, part of the whole group singing together, and engaging in an improvisation of words and movement.

The two boys are simultaneously the same and different, engaging in the same activity as the rest of the group (singing this particular song, sitting on the wooden steps together with the others) and noticeably different (they improvise words and movements). They are intra-acting with the group and intra-acting with each other, apprenticed, in Venn's (2002) terms, to both the group and each other, listening to the group and to each other. They are open to the music, which comes from outside them, and moves toward them. It penetrates them. It opens up in them as well as around them. Joshua's friend listens doubly to the sound of the whole group singing outside him and inside him, and he sees the movements, which become his movements too. He sings the words that he knows; the song he hears the group singing is also a song sung by him. At the same time he listens and watches Joshua's variations. He accepts those variations, demonstrating that acceptance with a hug, while still holding on to the same as the group for himself. But then he switches, taking up Joshua's variations as his own – a sextuple opening inside of which his "self" takes place. The two boys thus listen to each other and listen to the whole group; they are open to creative difference in the other, and in themselves even as they are enfolded together with the group of children in this moment of singing.

In Deleuze and Guattari's (1987) terms they stand on a familiar, safe plot of land (the song, the ritual, the place) and at the same time take off on their own line of flight (a transformative shift into the not-yet-known).

The two boys fold the group's song into themselves, and at the same time fold into each the innovative words and movements of the other. They also openly demonstrate love for each other and take a risk in being different. At the same time, the language of the song is Swedish, and the regular practice of singing together establishes music, and Swedish music in particular, as a significant element of being Swedish. It is a collectively learned way of enfolding oneself and being enfolded in the social fabric. The children's bodies are each archives of Swedish culture. As they sing together they accomplish their own stitching into the cultural fabric, its history, its language, its practices (Linnell, 2010). And while they do that they also accomplish a sense of themselves as different, as free to innovate within the terms of their culture, each listening to the other and taking up as their own the innovation that the other offers. Joshua enacts a facet of being made possible in this space, a space that he is, at the same time, performatively making real.

What it is possible for Joshua to *be* depends on what kind of subject is recognizable in this context, and on what that context affords him – how it positions him, what modes of enunciation it draws on, and what it values. He is simultaneously recognized in his specificity as a boy called Joshua, as a member of the four-year-olds, as a member of the singing group, and as a loving and innovative friend who explores being different. He differentiates himself.

What the preschool *is* depends, in turn, on how its members (which include Joshua) performatively accomplish it as a particular, recognizable place. The place exists in the moment of its production, whether that is in intra-actions among children, children with teachers and parents, adults with each other, intra-actions with the physical elements of the building and its pedagogical spaces and objects, or in the documentation of unfolding thoughts (Davies and Gannon, 2009).

Joshua's agency lies in his participation in the performative accomplishment, with others, of the openness of this place to the multiplicities of emergent, differentiating subjects accomplishing both this familiar place *and* new ways of being and knowing within it. Joshua exists in a context where what he is is understood both as specific and emergent, and where openness to new thought is the primary focus of the place itself.

Listening as a subject-as-intra-active-becoming opens up the possibility of valuing difference, not as categorical difference, but as an emergent, differentiating or becoming. Such listening involves stretching the ears, and all the senses. It requires a focused attention, an intensification of attention to the other, and to the happening in-between. This attention works through the most minute of details as neuroscientists have begun to find. In order to listen to another, they tell us, the neurons of the body must pick up, as a mirror, the being of the other, the minute details of sound and movement, of affect. Listening involves much more than the decoding of sound for meaning. It requires the orientation of the whole body toward the other. One's lips and tongue, for example, may work to shape in one's own mouth the sound one hears, as an integral part of coming to know or imagine what message the words carry. It is with mirror neurons that we appreciate, and experience for ourselves, the pain, or the joy, or the movement, or the sound of the other; we come to know the other through an intimate, social synaesthesia, where the words, the sonority, the affect of one are heard in the ears of the other, but also in their mouths, their eyes, their hearts, their gut (Bradshaw, 2009). We are not as separate as our thinking-as-usual leads us to think we are.

My final story in this chapter comes from my own community and involves Clementine, now three years old, and her mother Claudia. On this particular morning, Claudia and I had been outside chatting at the café, and I found myself mirroring her distress as she talked to me, and also mirroring Clementine's distress when Claudia raised her voice in reprimand. Later I wrote:

> Claudia was distracted by something Clementine was doing that she had asked her not to do. She raised her voice in reprimand, explaining to Clementine that she had been told not to do that. Clementine turned away from Claudia with her hands over her ears, looking toward the ground, quietly babbling. "She is doing that a lot lately. I know I shouldn't raise my voice – it's probably worse than letting the kids do whatever they are doing. I don't want them to annoy people, but I'm sure my raised voice is just as annoying, probably worse," she said. We talked about the complexity of raising children in an inner-city community, and I offered to have Clementine come to my place to do some painting.
>
> In the lift Clemmie, as usual, competently presses the button with 4 on it, to take us to the 4th floor. I ask as the lift takes off, thinking of the conversation with Claudia, "Is Mummy getting cross with you a lot lately?" She instantly puts her hands over her ears and turns away from me and starts babbling, just as she had in the coffee shop. I ask, "Is that what you do so you can't hear her?"
>
> "Yes," she says softly.
>
> "Do you know why she gets cross?"
>
> "No," she says.
>
> "Do you know she is cross because you are doing something that upsets her?"
>
> Clemmie looks at me, a little surprised, and says, "No".
>
> "Do you know you have got the power to stop her being cross, because what you do affects how Mummy feels? You can do things that make her happy, or you can do things that make her angry and sad." At that point we arrived at the 4th floor.
>
> At my door Clemmie points to the number on the door, as she always does, saying, "Two zero – twenty. Bronny's house". And we go in and turn our attention to painting. Several days later, Claudia tells me that when she had next raised her voice in reprimand, Clementine had taken hold of her hand and kissed it. Her anger had totally evaporated in the face of such a sweet and surprising action. I told, in turn, of the brief conversation we had had in the lift. We were both amazed at Clementine's capacity to listen, and to put such complex knowledge into practice in such a creative way.

Clementine and Claudia were caught in a repeated pattern that both of them found distressing – one positioned as angry mother and the other as naughty child. Claudia's strategy was to appeal to Clementine as an individualized identity, who must choose to transform her behaviour through an act of will. Implicitly, she must compare herself with an ideal subject and judge herself as falling short of that ideal, so developing as her own the desire to be different – to be well-behaved in just this way. Because of my emergent think-ing about listening, I could see another possibility, of approaching Clementine as a creatively evolving ~~subject~~, able to put herself up against thought where it is happening, and to expand thought and invent new ways of being-in-relation to her mother.

(In)conclusion

In this chapter I have extended Bergson's lines of descent and ascent to a dif-fractive play with self-as-identity and the ~~subject~~ intra-actively becoming. The repetitive self-as-identity I have defined as singular, and in terms of its will, and the ~~subject~~ intra-actively becoming as both singular and plural and in terms of its openness to new thought. I have argued that these two ways of being are in creative tension with each other, the latter having to grapple with the conserva-tism of the former in order to become or remain open to difference, to become different, to engage in differentiation. The child learning to play the triangle was repelled by the wild experimentation of her peers. But she learned from watching and listening to them how to make her triangle sing, and so was able to take off on a line of flight with the teacher and the piano and the triangle. The stories of Joshua reveal the ways in which he is simultaneously singular and plural, emergent in relation to his classmates, the teacher and his mother, and the familiar striations of life at preschool, while simultaneously inventing a new line of flight for himself and his friend to engage in. And finally, through listening to Clementine, we can see the lines of descent that might lock an angry mother and naughty child into painfully repetitive lines of descent, in which neither can bear to hear the other; and emerging from those striations, the unfolding of a new thought, opening up new ways of hearing each other, new ways of being in relation to each other.

In the next chapter I encounter an experience of anger between two boys at Trollet, and in a diffractive engagement with that anger I extend the thought I have engaged in here to include some aspects of zen buddhism, which has interesting intersections with Deleuzian thought. Listening when things go wrong, when the usual striations are not working to keep everyone predictable and safe, opens up the possibility of a line of flight – the emergence of a new thought that is trying to make itself heard (Readings, 1996).

Note

1 The line through the word "subject" is a deconstructive line. It signals that while the concept of the subject is one we cannot do without, it is locked in a series of binaries, and hierarchies within those binaries, that need to be pulled undone. The individual subject is not singular *or* plural, not self *or* other, not fixed *or* mobile, but all of these.

Chapter 4

Reading anger in early childhood intra-actions

Conflict can lead to a hardening of lines of descent and to increased regulation of the participants to bring them into line within the existing striations. It may also lead to a questioning of some of our taken-for-granted ways of thinking and being. In this chapter I explore a clash between two five-year-old boys at Trollet, which took place over a period of two weeks. Trollet is an extraordinarily harmonious place, where moments of anger are rare. When anger erupted between Jonathan and Tom it caught my attention, demanding that I search for ways to extend my thinking and my capacity to listen. I found their anger distressing – it affected me. The anger was not confined in individual bodies, it flowed in-between, affecting us all.

I begin with an extended series of observations of the two boys, and then diffractively open out the space of thought about anger, its embodiment, its epistemologies, and its ethics.

Jonathan and Tom

It is the beginning of the preschool year. Jonathan is new to the preschool. He knows the other five-year-old boys from playing football with them at the weekends. The other boys have been together at this preschool since they were babies and have formed a strong, mutually supportive group.

> Monday. Outside play. It is Jonathan's first day. He has joined Tom's group and is playing bandy[1] in the small amphitheatre. There are four five-year-old boys playing. They are totally immersed in the game, which appears to be chaotic, yet they all seem to know what they are doing. Several balls and their sticks are flying high and fast and furious. Each smack of the ball against the wall is greeted with a loud "Jo!" by the one who hit it. The ball often hits the bodies of the other boys as they fly to get another ball, but they do not appear to register that they have been hit. Suddenly Tom drops out. Dejected, walking slowly toward the surrounding stairs, a ball hits him in the ankle and he scowls, but does not say anything. He sits on the stairs and watches the game.

It is not unusual for children to sit out for a while when they are hurt and then join back in. And it is also not unusual for one to quit and for all to follow suit. Tom's scowl makes it clear that he is angry with one of the other boys. The game continues without him. There is a great deal of excitement combined with a sense of danger. Tom's scowl sets him aside from the group's pleasure in the game.

> Suddenly Jonathan calls a halt, and the game stops. The boys stand in a circle and Jonathan tosses his stick high. It falls behind him, far out of the amphitheatre. No teacher notices – there is no reprimand. Jonathan runs off, calling Osvald's name and they flock after him. They go to the sandbox, which is full of dinosaurs and lions and tigers. Tom seems to be now once more fully engaged. There is a great deal of urgent verbal negotiation, then Tom moves off quietly to play alone in the fort close by, watching from a distance.

It is only day one, but the movement of the group seems to position the new boy, Jonathan, as a shining centre of gravity. The tossing of his stick is read by the boys as heroic, and a signal of his superiority in playing bandy, even if (and perhaps because) it is dangerous and would be disapproved of by teachers. Taking risks is integral to dominant masculinity and to the evident excitement of their play. The boys risked being hurt by the sticks or the ball when they were playing, and Jonathan risked getting into trouble with the teachers when he threw his stick. Tom, who used to be a leader in the group, has, at least temporarily, lost that position as the flow of energy circles around Jonathan. For a second time he removes himself from the group and watches unhappily.

The intensity and excitement flowing around Jonathan is palpable. The boys flow around him and after him, and Tom is cast up like flotsam of wrecked friendships. Whereas Tom was once a vital force among this group of boys, he is now isolated and angry, and yet still trying to recreate the old patterns of engagement:

> Tom comes back closer to the boys in the sandpit. He calls Osvald's name and runs off, just as Jonathan had done earlier in the movement from amphitheatre to sandpit. The boys stay put in the sandpit as if they didn't hear him. He tries again, but again the boys ignore him. Jonathan then initiates a movement in the opposite direction to the small playhouse and the boys flock after him. They take the dinosaurs with them and Tom comes too. (There are two small adjacent playhouses with outdoor cooking and digging areas). Jonathan, Osvald and Kent go inside. Tom is outside cooking. Osvald comes out to paint the roof of the house (with paintbrush and water). The other two boys are now inside chatting, negotiating their roles in the family. Suddenly Jonathan leads all the boys, including Tom, running off into the forest. Then they flock back to the small house very excited.

There is apparently some creature (a spider?) on the ceiling and they start throwing things at it – saucepans and dinosaurs. The teacher intervenes, telling them not to throw things. The danger of whatever it was seems to evaporate. Three boys settle down to talk and Osvald continues to paint the roof. Jonathan seems to be taking the lead in the inside chatting. Osvald is father. Jonathan is 72 and his "brother" Tom is zero. Nothing. Nothing is repeated. Osvald stops painting to fill his paint bucket. Tom comes outside and takes up Osvald's brush and begins to paint. Osvald does not object but calmly continues to fill up his paint bucket. In contrast to Osvald, who applied evident skill in wielding the brush, Tom is quite awkward. Kent comes out and tells him he can't paint because he is zero. Nothing. Tom says he wants to be the older brother. He abandons the brush, however, saying that painting is, after all, boring. Osvald resumes painting. At this point the children ask me and the teacher (who has been translating for me) to go away, and we leave, respecting their right not to be observed.

As their play continues, the boys are clearly engaging in the production of contempt toward Tom (Søndergaard, 2012). He oscillates between sulky with-drawal and struggling to regain the familiar position of one who is liked and respected. But the abjection of him seems to be gathering momentum. Against his will he is being assigned the position of baby and nothingness.

Søndergaard analyses the condition that she calls social exclusion anxiety as a characteristic feature of children who find themselves being bullied. Social exclusion anxiety

> builds on the social psychological concept of human beings as existentially dependent on social embeddedness . . . This point is highlighted [in this analysis of bullying] in order to focus on the anxiety that arises when social embeddedness is jeopardised and the hope and longing to be part of a com-munity is threatened.
>
> (Søndergaard, 2012: 5)

The concerted abjection of Tom taking place in this moment can be read as the usual rough and tumble of children's play, and in this sense as causing no real harm. The teachers seem interested rather than alarmed. Jonathan's mother is there observing, paid by the Swedish government to take time off work to help her child settle into his new school. She looks surprised when I comment to her that Jonathan is surprisingly at the centre of things for a boy who has just arrived. She appears not to find the children's play at all interesting.

But the abjection of Tom can also be read as verging on the unbearable. It is not just Jonathan who is humiliating him, but also the circle of friends who have, until now, been allied with him. Like Joshua in Chapter 3, Tom and his friends have intra-actively created a communal space in which they accomplish who they are and who it is possible to be. He has depended on his alliance with them for a viable life (Butler, 2004), but that alliance, through these intra-active encounters, is being decomposed, just as the alliance between the two small boys and a girl scaling the rock face in Chapter 1 was decomposed.

It is possible that Tom's refusal to acknowledge Jonathan's position as shining centre of gravity threatens the possibility of the alliance functioning success-fully in this new and exciting moment of collectively becoming-friends-with-Jonathan. It seems that the boys who long to be Jonathan's friend, to intra-act with him such that they too can be skilful and shining, cannot easily accom-modate Tom's angry withdrawals, which would pull them away from Jonathan and break up the newly forming alliance. The fact that the teacher and I were asked to go away and no longer serve as possible witnesses to what was going on suggests that the boys knew very well that the decomposition of old alliances was dangerous – more dangerous than we, as observers, realized at the time.

> Tuesday. Outside play. Four boys and a girl are running in a flock through the forest. Tom, looking very unhappy, is running after them, but is far behind. They run through the forest and round the perimeter of the play-ground, and it seems hopeless – he will never catch up. I don't know what has happened but I feel he has been somehow tricked into following. He looks as if he believes he will catch up if he tries hard enough, and the flock of children looks triumphant, as though it knows he never will. He looks exhausted. I feel deeply concerned for him.

I begin to feel extreme exclusion anxiety as I watch Tom running and as I see the triumph in the others that he is managing to ignore. His exclusion has become unbearable to watch. I catch myself falling into a familiar line of descent, individualizing the problem and blaming Jonathan. I want someone to tell Jonathan: *this is not how the children behave here.* Even though Jonathan is clearly not acting alone, my outrage on behalf of Tom leads me straight into this judgemental, individualizing categorization of Jonathan, blaming an indi-vidual as the cause of another's pain. I want the painful treatment of Tom to stop.

I decide that I have to talk to Birgitta about what is going on. But far from joining in the practice of blaming Jonathan, she responds to my account by telling me how important it is for the teachers working with a Reggio-Emilia-inspired philosophy to listen to each child and to find something special about them. In that same week I give a lecture to all the teachers in this preschool and in neighbouring preschools, and I talk about the trouble brewing among the boys, and the different possible ways of reading it and responding to it. What I notice in the days that follow is that, more than usual, the teachers are casually stopping and listening to individual children. I especially notice Jonathan's face shining as he looks up at a teacher and talks to her in response to her question. I also notice a more concerted effort to regulate their play, insisting, for exam-ple, that bandy sticks must not be swung above shoulder height. Rather than

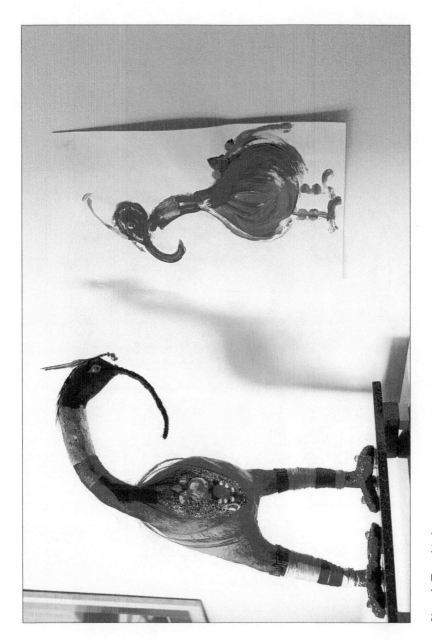

Plate I Two birds

Plate 2 Angry spider mother

Plate 3 Response to spider mother I

Plate 4 Response to spider mother 2

Plate 5 Mermaids with spots

Plate 6 Mermaids in hospital

Plate 7 Mermaids in park

Plate 8 Mermaids ice-skating

Plate 9 Hair blowing in wind I

Plate 10 Hair blowing in wind 2

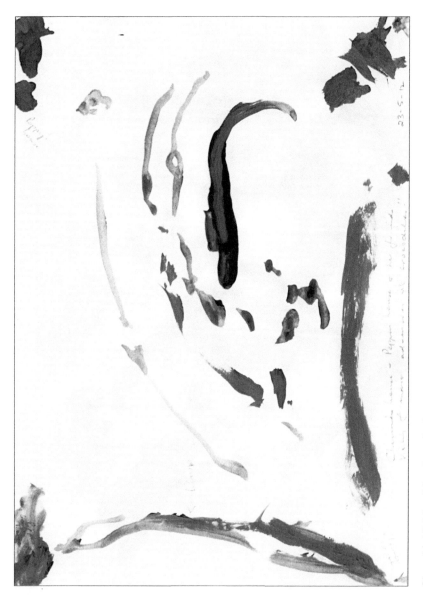

Plate 11 Visiting friends and adventures

Plate 12 Clouds

Plate 13 Birth of Sunday

Plate 14 Mermaid family

Plate 15 Poppies I

Plate 16 Poppies 2

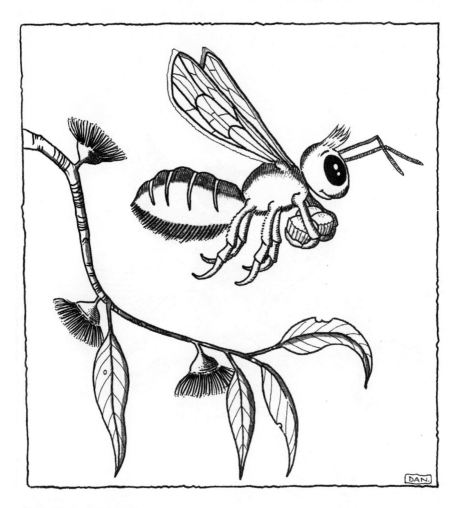

Plate 17 Leaf-cutter Bee

Plate 18 Kookaburra and Fairy

standing apart and observing, and only stepping in when called on, they begin
to join in more, both playing as team members and supervising the implemen-
tation of the rules of soccer and bandy. The "trouble", however, continues to
unfold.

> Thursday. Outside play. Joshua, Osvald, Tom and the twins are up on top
> of the big rock in the forest. Jonathan, alone, walks casually toward them.
> He has put on his royal-blue jacket with his hood up and his arms out of
> the sleeves. He looks like a mythical hero. He stays near the edge of the
> group. Suddenly he wrestles with William to take his very nice stick away
> from him. William loses the battle. Jonathan leaps up onto the centre of
> the big rock, lithe and skilful in his movements, challenging the others
> to a sword fight. William retreats behind a rock where the other boys
> can't see him, and weeps at the loss of his beautiful stick. After a while he
> wipes his eyes and begins looking for another stick. Jonathan enters into
> fierce and exciting sword battle with Osvald with all the others watching
> and shouting. A teacher comes to speak to them and the scene suddenly
> dissolves.

At the beginning of Thursday's observation, Tom was back at the centre of
his group with Jonathan outside. Jonathan casually enhanced his image with a
dramatic blue hooded cape and a magnificent stick. His superior athletic skills
were evident as he leapt on to the large rock and challenged Osvald to a duel.
Once again the play was both exciting and dangerous, and drew on images of
heroic masculinity that boys everywhere are encouraged to admire. No matter that the teachers don't like it – it may even be that that increases its value
and excitement. Jonathan has shown that he can rapidly move from outside to
centre, and that this group of boys will welcome him.

> Monday. Outside play. The boys are playing soccer. Jonathan calls "Jo!"
> loudly when he kicks a goal. Then Tom kicks a goal and suddenly he and
> Jonathan crash into each other and fall down in a tangle of arms and legs.
> Tom stays on the ground. Jonathan runs away off the soccer field and stops
> to look back as if scared. Tom gets up and runs in the opposite direction,
> over to the fence under the oak trees. He begins to climb the paling fence
> as if to run away from the preschool. The teacher calls him, then goes after
> him. The soccer game has dissolved itself. She encourages the two boys to
> talk to each other. Tom cannot stop crying. He is outraged. She takes him
> by the hand and takes him inside. Tom talks to her all the way, pouring
> out his story.
>   Later. Tom is still angry. He is yelling at Jonathan over at the small cab-
> ins. A teacher has her arm around him, sitting beside him, but he will not
> stop yelling. It seems he believes Jonathan deliberately tripped him up on
> the soccer field and he is intent on revenge.

Tom's rage toward Jonathan had been ignited by the accidental collision. The teacher showed compassion for him, listening to him, but his rage spilled over and kept spilling without apparent end. The collision had seemed to me to be an accident, but it has transformed Tom's tears and sullen withdrawal into a raging torrent. Jonathan has displayed the apparent power to abject Tom, though he could not have done that without the collusion of the other boys. Tom had lost his one-time power to initiate the movement of the group of boys, and not only could he no longer trust his friends to include him, but even his rare moment of glory in kicking a goal was taken away from him. He had experienced a profound loss of agency. He had no power over the flow of movement, and he had no power to stop the flow moving against him at any moment. His pain was so great that he attempted to escape the preschool, but was pulled back into the scene of his torment.

And where was Jonathan? He was clearly afraid – afraid perhaps of being blamed, of being seen as the cause of Tom's rage. Afraid perhaps of seeing himself and being seen as having got it wrong in this new place. He too was afraid of social exclusion. As Søndergaard (2012) explains, social exclusion anxiety is not an emotion that is experienced only by the ones who are excluded. It drives everyone to find ways to ensure their own continuing inclusion – in effect, their own existence as social beings.

Each one of these boys knew, though not necessarily consciously, that the production of contempt and abjection could turn toward him – that his capacity to endure depended on maintaining his embeddedness in the group. Excluding someone else, in this case Tom, is a common way of attempting to ensure one's own survival. As Søndergaard points out, however, it is a risky and fraught strategy, since the more social exclusion is practised the greater the fear each participant feels about his own exclusion, and the more motivated he may feel to ensure that it is someone else who is being excluded. This dynamic generally lies under or beyond conscious thought and is lodged in the affective flows between subjects and their encounters with each other.

There were times during the weeks of observation that I noticed Jonathan's exhaustion. His lips were dry as if he was badly dehydrated, and in class he barely participated. At the end of the second week, at lunch, Tom seemed to have regained some of his ascendancy, humorously challenging everyone at his table to wrap their arms around the back of their heads and reach their fingers into their mouths.

> Friday. After lunch, Tom placed himself strategically near the door out into the playground, waiting for the others to come out. At just the right moment he called for them all to go to the carpentry area and ran toward it. They followed and began busily hammering nails and pulling them out of two large logs. Instead of using their hammers as levers, they were pulling back, using the weight and strength of their bodies to extract the nails. Jonathan's nail suddenly came out and he fell over backwards hitting his

head. In that moment all his strength evaporated and he cried and cried as if his world had collapsed, and nothing could comfort him. The teacher held him, and in front of all the others, he sobbed again and again that he wanted his mother. The other boys, including Tom, watched out of the corner of their eyes, quietly concerned. They kept on hammering and pulling out nails, waiting for him to recover and return to them.

These two moments of rage, brim-full of despair, once documented in this kind of detail, once discussed and analysed, demand something more than usual. They demand the extension of thought – "trying to hear that which cannot be said but which tries to make itself heard" (Readings, 1996: 165). Tom's rage does not *belong* solely to Tom. It does not originate *in* Tom. It comes to exist in the intra-action between Tom and the other boys – in the interface where Tom affects and is affected by the others. Tom is overwhelmed by the fact that his survival among his friends is at stake. It is both an ontological wave of fear and anger that he experiences *and*, inextricably, it is epistemological. He makes sense of what is happening by attributing his exclusion to Jonathan. At the same time his withdrawal and his subsequent expression of rage impacts on the others and their emotions but also their perceptions – of themselves and of Tom.

But what of the ethical dimension?

I had been very moved by the children's quiet concern at Jonathan's despair. It reminded me of the yoga lesson that Christina had taught earlier in the week in the main square of the preschool, where children as young as three took up for themselves the calm, meditative possibility that yoga offered them. I also remember the dramatic and transformative effect that a new way of thinking had on Clementine's intra-actions with Claudia when Claudia was angry in Chapter 3. I began to wonder about the possibilities of children mobilizing mindfulness as a way of responding to the experience of anger.

Imagining anger differently

Anh's Anger (Silver and Krömer, 2009) is a children's story inspired by the buddhist teacher Thich Nhat Hanh (2001), in which a boy uses mindfulness in order to make friends with his anger:

> The small boy Anh is angry with his grandfather for insisting that it is time for dinner. He shouts at his grandfather, telling him he hates him. He cries and, in a rage, he destroys the block castle he had been so happily building.
>
> His grandfather says to him, calmly, "You are upset. Please go to your room and sit with your anger. I'll come when you are calm and able to talk". Anh runs to his room.
>
> He feels his anger growing bigger and bigger. Then it appears as a red hairy creature, who says, "Finally, I was hoping you would notice me". Anh asks if the creature is his anger and the creature nods.

Anh and the creature talk, and Anh listens carefully to what his anger has to say and to how he feels in the anger's presence. They shout and whirl and drum on the floor together until they are exhausted, and then they sit silently, in a meditation position, breathing in and out, focusing on their breath.

The creature begins to shrink. They talk to each other as friends, and the now much smaller red creature smiles at Anh. They breathe some more and Anh begins to feel better. The creature has vanished.

Grandfather knocks at the door and they sit together, Anh enfolded in his grandfather's arms.

Anh, with the new insight he has gained from listening to his anger, apologizes for shouting and explains that he was angry because he wanted to keep playing. His grandfather thanks him for his kind words and tells him, "You took good care of your anger and it went away". The story ends with the grandfather telling a story of himself being angry when he was a small boy.

"Taking good care" in this story meant that Anh, with the help of his grandfather, notices "I am angry". He then acknowledges his anger, expresses it, listens to it, and makes friends with it. Rather than judging or dismissing himself or his emotions, he asks what it is his anger has to tell him – about why he is angry, and what he needs to do in response. Anh's anger tells him two simple things: he wanted, unreasonably, to finish his castle before dinner, and that he needed to apologize to his grandfather for his hurtful words. The negative intensity was transformed into positive intensity through careful and attentive listening, and also through meditation. Anh could have remained caught in the rage and antagonism toward his grandfather, but through a combination of listening, receptivity, and openness to an encounter with his own anger he could move the situation from a stuck place toward something new – a not-yet-known encounter with his grandfather.

In marked contrast, in dominant educational discourses, being sent to one's room, or to the time-out room, depends on a reading of the child in terms of self-as-identity. The child must learn to *desire* being good, which s/he will, once deprived of what s/he wants (to be with others and accepted). From a cognitivist perspective, the child will come to understand that the behaviour is undesirable and will no longer *choose* to engage in it. Either way the anger will be extinguished, rather than transformed, through a rational act of will (Laws, 2011; Laws and Davies, 2000).

From a buddhist perspective, the anger, as Thich Nhat Hanh (2001) explains it, is negative energy, but it is not to be expelled or extinguished. It must be listened to, and made friends with, in such a way that it is transformed into positive energy, much as garbage or compost can be transformed into a garden of flowers or vegetables. Anh is sent to his bedroom to provide the space in which that transformation can occur. This is not a moral judgement against

Anh or his anger, but opening up a space in which Anh can embrace both himself and his anger.

From this perspective, compassion for one's raging self, and compassion for the one who has been harmed by the rage, are life giving. From this perspective, while anger may be toxic and harmful to everyone concerned, we all experience it, so moral judgement is not the point. Rather, the practices of mindfulness and listening with compassion and without judgement transform the negative energy and enable Anh and his grandfather to embrace each other with loving kindness. Anh apologizes to his grandfather and his grandfather thanks him. This is interestingly similar to Birgitta's response to hearing about Tom's anger and about my social exclusion anxiety on his behalf. Each must be listened to attentively; each is of value. The mindfulness practices and the Reggio-Emilia-inspired practices are interestingly similar to Deleuzian ethics, as discussed in Chapter 1.

In the dominant western narratives of anger there is a doubled judgement – of oneself and of the other. Anger is not usually judged to be a good emotion to have or to express (unless one is "getting it out" and thus getting rid of it, or unless it can be justified as warranted on moral grounds – such as Christ's anger at the money-changers in the temple). Holding on to anger, however, and dwelling on it may well lead to an endless loop of accusation, retaliation, defence, and fresh accusation. One's antagonist (and each, in all probability, regards the other as the antagonist) is judged as bad for having provoked the anger. A false binary is set up between the angry one who is wounded, and the guilty one who is the supposed source of the anger. The angry one may be consumed with self-righteous rage that is turned toward the other. The anger is difficult to resolve, since its energy goes on being enlivened through the narrative of wounds, guilt, and revenge. And revenge, as Butler observes, can never be fully satisfied:

> It is always possible to say, "Oh, some violence was done to me, and this gives me full permission to act under the sign of 'self-defence'". Many atrocities are committed under the sign of a "self-defence" that, precisely because it achieves a permanent moral justification for retaliation, knows no end and can have no end. Such a strategy has developed an infinite way to rename its aggression as suffering and so provides infinite justification for its aggression.
>
> (Butler, 2005: 100–101)

The self-defence narrative, imbricated in the judgemental framework that Deleuze calls morality, can lead to an ongoing rage that appears to be locked in, causing oneself, and the others involved, physical and psychological damage. Underpinning this narrative is the bounded conception of self and other as identifiable entities. The one who harms and the one who is harmed are distinct and separate, and the original aggressive act can be *identified*.

Ethics, in contrast, is intra-active and open to the unknown in the other; it involves an openness and attention to the details of each present moment:

> [Justice] entails acknowledgement, recognition, [and] . . . the ongoing practice of being open and alive to each meeting, each intra-action, so that we might use our ability to respond, our responsibility, to help awaken, to breathe life into ever new possibilities for living justly. The world and its possibilities for becoming are remade in each meeting. How then shall we understand our role in helping constitute who and what come to matter?
>
> (Barad, 2007: x)

There are fascinating parallels between zen buddhist philosophy and Deleuzian thought. While the language they choose makes them at first glance appear to be saying the opposite to each other, there are some intriguing points of commonality. Both are interested in how we can enable ourselves to think the unthinkable, in the necessity of thinking for oneself instead of being driven by imposed rules, and both are committed to dismantling the ego/self as a fixed unitary entity.

The Deleuzian approach is to generate movement beyond fixed places by finding ways to think the unthinkable. Deleuze generated new concepts, not as an epistemology to impose on, or explain, being, but as a generative practice that might unlock automatic lines of descent. Drawing as well on affects and percepts, he explored ways to rethink human subjects not as bounded entities but as intersecting lines of force or intensity, where *"each living thing – each individual – is a contraction of the world, a connection with all of the world"* (Williams, 2003: 23). Buddhist thought similarly distrusts those concepts that hold us in repeated lines of descent. It emphasizes percepts and affects as a means of discovering ways to think the unthinkable, and finding ways to be in the world as a particular manifestation of that world, and in connection with all of the world.

Just as Deleuzian philosophy locates life in differentiation and lines of ascent, zen buddhism tells us to give up our habituated and usual ways of thinking, to abandon our egos and our attachments, both material and emotional, and to find in the consequent *emptiness* a truth of ourselves. That truth is not so much an individualized truth as the discovery that lying beyond (and before) all the illusions of self-as-identity is a Buddha-self that we have, or are, in common. It enjoins us to work tirelessly and for years if necessary, with relentless self-discipline, to achieve an effortless letting go of illusory truths. In that letting go each can empty the self, not in order to accomplish an imagined good, but in order to become what each of us was already: "one does not practice Zen to become a Buddha; one practices it because one is a Buddha from the beginning – and this 'original realization' is the starting point of Zen life" (Watts, 1957: 154).

Both buddhist and Deleuzian thought emphasize the importance of the knower experiencing and experimenting for her- or himself, breaking loose from fixed ways of knowing and being. In zen life emptiness and fullness, strug-gling and letting go, all binaries in fact, are to be understood not as opposites but as complementaries, where neither can exist without the other. Watts tells a story to illustrate this point taken from Eugen Herrigal's (1953) *Zen in the Art of Archery*, where intentionality and spontaneity are integrally related:

> Herrigal spent almost five years trying to find the right way of releasing the bowstring, for it had to be done "unintentionally," in the same way as a ripe fruit bursts its skin. His problem was to resolve the paradox of practic-ing relentlessly without ever "trying," and to let go of the taut string inten-tionally without intention. His master at one and the same time urged him to keep on working and working, but also to stop making an effort. For the art cannot be learned unless the arrow "shoots itself," unless the string is released *wu-hsin* and *wu-nien*, without "mind" and without blocking, or choice. After all those years of practice there came a day when it just hap-pened – how, or why, Herrigal never understood.
>
> (Watts, 1957: 195–196)

I have been reading (and more recently writing with) Deleuze for over a decade now, not knowing where his often inaccessible and complex writing might take me, but happy to go there nonetheless. Understanding Deleuze is a struggle. It takes time, and the concepts only work if you experience them for yourself. There comes a point where the ideas release themselves, almost like Herrigal's arrow. Deleuze takes you into the not-yet-known, the not-yet-thinkable, where one must forget, and let go, in order to open up to the new.

Both zen buddhism and Deleuzian philosophy wish the subject to move beyond mindless, habitual repetitive citations toward what buddhism calls mindfulness and toward what Deleuze calls thought, or lines of flight. Bud-dhism sees "mindlessness" as filled with concepts and clichéd repetitions, and as obedient to authoritarian knowledges. The move to mindfulness, in buddhist terms, is one that involves letting go of concepts and authority *and* trusting the body's own knowledge gained through repeating, in a disciplined way, the buddhist verses and gathas that inform buddhist practice. Deleuze, in a compa-rable move, sees mindless habitual citations as creating both an illusion of stasis *and* providing a "safe plot of land" from which it is possible to take off on a new line of flight (Davies and Gannon, 2009). This flight, facilitated by the concepts he has generated, he sees as emergent, or immanent. It involves invention as well as letting go of what went before. The creatively evolving Deleuzian sub-ject, the subject open to the not-yet-known, is the place where new thought happens, those thoughts having the power to generate new ways of being.

Deleuze argued that the self, a concept that evokes self primarily as an entity, as separate or finite matter, is a misleading and erroneous way of conceiving of what it is to be human. He was interested in thinking of human subjects as movement, as made up of intersecting lines of force where matter and force are not separable. The problem of imagining the self, he says, as a separate finite entity places an unnecessary limitation on the internal life of the self as it shapes itself to fit the requirements of logic and of language. The imagined self as a stable entity is one that may take a great deal of effort to work against, since the struggle is not only against logic and language but also against the others who are caught within it.

Thich Nhat Hanh wrote in his early memoirs of being a buddhist monk of this same struggle with loved ones who wanted to keep him the same:

> To live we must die every instant. We must perish again and again in the storms that make life possible. It would be better, I thought, if everyone cast me from their thoughts. I cannot be a human being and, at the same time, be an unchanging object of love or hatred, annoyance or devotion. I must continue to grow . . . I cannot force myself back into the shell I've just broken out of. This is a source of great loneliness for me.
>
> (1998: 87)

This tension between habitual practice and the spontaneous emergence of something new is a continuing theme in both buddhist and Deleuzian thought and practice. Although buddhist practitioners are enjoined to engage in rituals and techniques involving the repetition of words from authoritative others, the Buddha-self is spontaneous, and un-self-conscious. It comes from "the unthinkable ingenuity and creative power of man's spontaneous and natural functioning – a power which is blocked when one tries to master it in terms of formal methods and techniques" (Watts, 1957: 26). The techniques are only useful as an instrument, not as the experience itself. One must experiment with life, and not simply follow the already known path. Buddhist practice, like Herrigal's years of practice with the bow and arrow, may or may not lead to the spontaneous, un-self-conscious arrow's flight, or the experience of one's Buddha-self.

Deleuze explores this same shift as a non-judgemental openness to oneself and the other. To greet the other ethically, one asks, simply, "What is it to be this?" What makes the just-thisness of you, in this moment?

> You ask yourself how is that possible? How is this possible in an internal way? In other words, you relate the thing or the statement to the mode of existence that it implies, that it envelops in itself. How must it be in order to say that? Which manner of Being does this imply? You seek the enveloped modes of existence, and not the transcendent values.
>
> (Deleuze, 1980: np)

Thich Nhat Hanh expresses a related thought when he says: "If we only analyze someone from the outside, without becoming one with them, without entering their shoes, their skin, we will never really understand them" (2010: 32).

In both Deleuzian and buddhist thought, it is the construction of oneself as ego or self-as-entity that closes down the capacity to see the world in oneself and the other. One becomes caught up in categorical difference and in illusions of fixity. In Deleuzian terms, fixity seeks to contain and to give direction through already existing striations. It seeks to coerce each individual to move in limited paths in order to make them more amenable to government (that is, government of oneself by oneself, in the name of morality and self-survival, and government by the other in the name of a particular order). The material/discursive habit of being-oneself-as-ego is limiting, and yet it is a difficult habituation to give up. Deleuze talks of a philosophical war, a war without battles, with and against oneself and with and against those governmental forces in oneself: "philosophy can't battle with the powers that be, but it fights a war without battles, a guerrilla campaign against them . . . Since the powers aren't just external things, but permeate each of us, philosophy throws us all into constant negotiations with, and a guerrilla campaign against, ourselves" (Deleuze, 1995: np).

Thich Nhat Hanh similarly writes of a guerrilla campaign in which one catches oneself in the act of being taken over by the thoughts and practices that permeate us. He is interested in figuring how to let them go, how to exist without them, or in the face of them. His teachings are, he says, "tools which we can use to shatter and demolish our habitual and troublesome ways of thinking, old habits forged by our everyday lives" (2010: 55). His guerrilla campaign is based on love – one must love the enemy in order to know and overcome it, whether that enemy is outside oneself or inside oneself. One should not rush to judgement, but take up a position of mindful, compassionate knowing in which it becomes clear that the enemy is not so very different from the self. Compassion toward oneself is intrinsic to Thich Nhat Hanh's mindfulness. In dealing with our own anger, for example, we might care for it like an old friend, or a baby:

> mindfulness is touching, recognizing, greeting, and embracing [the anger]. It does not fight or suppress. The role of mindfulness is like the role of the mother, embracing and soothing the suffering child. Anger is in you; anger is your baby, your child. You have to take very good care of it. When it recognizes anger, mindfulness says, "Hello there, my anger, I know you are there. I will take good care of you, don't worry."
>
> (Thich Nhat Hanh, 2001: 119)

This loving, gentle, almost humorous approach is not about accepting all that is in order to keep it the same. It is an act of love that sees the interdependence of all beings, and all aspects of being. One sees the other in oneself and oneself in the other, and opens up new understandings that have the power to transform both. Through mindfulness one comes to understand that some cultural patterns, when they dominate our ways of being, can become toxic if we allow them to remain fixed. The individualized ego is one form which that fixity can take.

The individualized ego, in buddhist thought, is constructed not through compassion and love, but through judgement, through comparison, through categorization, and through the fear of being found lacking. Individualism appears to offer the ego freedom, but it is only if you are this or that kind of person who has rid him- or herself from certain aspects that are judged to be negative that you can be loved and accepted. The self-as-identity, or ego, tends therefore to suppress and deny the negative in itself, rather than, as Thich Nhat Hanh recommends, accepting it and treating it with love.

The idea of the ego as a fixed entity, that both buddhist and Deleuzian thought work against, is strung together out of a series of moments or events, which together take on an illusion of being solid, of being *this* and definitely not *that*. In buddhist thought

> the ego exists in an abstract sense alone, being an abstraction from memory, somewhat like the illusory circle of fire made by a whirling torch. We can, for example, imagine the path of a bird through the sky as a distinct line which it has taken. But this line is as abstract as a line of latitude. In concrete reality the bird left no line, and, similarly, the path from which our ego is abstracted has entirely disappeared. Thus any attempt to cling to the ego or to make it an effective source of action is doomed to frustration.
>
> (Watts, 1957: 47)

In both buddhist and Deleuzian thought the egoic self is dissolved. The human subject cannot readily be separated from the intensities or lines of force that make it up (or that it makes up) at any one moment. The distinction between one human and another, between human and animal, between human and earth other, cannot be sustained. What characterizes one being at any one point in time are the particular intensities running through that being, intensities and forces that may run through others, though differently configured at any one time. Categories for sorting different kinds of beings, and different individuals in this conception of being, are not so useful. Deleuze observes: "It's not a question of being this or that sort of human, but of . . . unravelling your body's human organization, exploring this or that zone of bodily intensity, with everyone discovering their own particular zones, and the groups, populations, species that inhabit them" (1995: 11).

If we think of Tom and Jonathan in the terms that have emerged in this conceptual detour into zen and Deleuzian thought, then we could say Tom was run through with the intensities of fear and anger. That intensity of fear, and the social exclusion anxiety, became intensities that ran through the others as well. They were being formed by the same intensities, while Tom was limited by a mode of thinking about himself and his anger that divided him and Jonathan against each other. From the beginning he located the problem – the cause of his misery – inside Jonathan. He excluded himself. He blamed the other.

But what if, when he first walked away from the bandy amphitheatre, he had been able to intra-act with his anger as an old familiar friend? What if he could have trusted himself and his anger and said, "Hello there my old friend, I will take good care of you" (Thich Nhat Hanh, 2001)? What if he could have asked his anger what it had to tell him about the intensities of fear and outrage? What strategies might he have mobilized out there on the playground to acknowledge his rage, to talk to it, and listen to it carefully? Could he have engaged in mindful breathing sitting out there on the steps? Could he have looked at Jonathan with compassion, as a new boy who is on the outside and must be helped to make his way in? Or might he have heard, if he had listened to his anger, that there was something terribly wrong unfolding in the dynamics of his group which needed addressing with the help of the teachers?

And what of Jonathan? He was caught up in the intra-actively exciting drama of taking centre place with this new group of boys. He was able to engage to his heart's content in all the physical games he was so good at, unlike at his previous preschool. At the same time, he was exhausted and afraid. Perhaps his own experience of social exclusion anxiety was intense in these first two weeks at his new preschool, and Tom's opposition and anger intensified that anxiety. His management of the exciting flow of boys together was interrupted by Tom's angry withdrawals and by the occasional reprimands of the teachers. He managed the flow of intra-actions around him by excluding and abjecting Tom. It was difficult to see his anxiety because he was so skilled at sport and imaginative play. The signs were small at first – his white dry lips, his silence in class – and finally they were terribly evident in his sobbing, inconsolable body.

(In)conclusion

The question that emerges, then, is not who was to blame, but who and what came to matter? I have explored here the intersecting ontology, epistemology, and ethics of anger in preschool children and I am curious now about what concepts and what bodily knowledge Jonathan and Tom would need in order to look at each other with compassion, not driven by social exclusion anxiety, but by a shared sense of social justice. Social justice, as Barad (2007: x) describes it, has at its heart the ongoing practice of "being open and alive to each intra-action" and asking, "How then shall we understand our role in helping constitute who and what come to matter?" Is this, I wonder, an ethical responsibility children can begin to take up at an early age, as they endlessly explore the emergent possibilities of being in the playground? The quiet, non-judgemental concern on the faces of the boys when Jonathan was crying suggests to me that they can. So that is an exciting direction that this diffractive analysis might take off in as this research evolves its own lines of flight.

Pushing up against the edges of thought about anger, my initial reading of the anger expressed by the two boys morphed from one in which I first read the scene with habitual thoughts-as-usual, mobilizing concepts of guilt and blame, into a more ethical encounter with the rage of the two boys, in which

I began to be able to ask, with Deleuze, and with Thich Nhat Hanh, what is it to be this? And how does it work? Listening to them in a set of diffractive movements I found a new question emerging about what children are capable of as they intra-act with each other in the playground. Can they learn to look at themselves and each other with compassion rather than judgement? What encounters with teachers, and with each other, would help to open up this possibility? Can they learn to recognize the affective intensity of social exclusion anxiety as it runs through their collective bodies, and work not to reiterate normative judgements and exclusions but invent, with the teacher, a new collective refrain, opening up their affective commitment to listening, to receptivity, and to thought? Can they learn to listen with compassion to their own and each other's fear and anger? Such learning could begin quite simply with learning to notice one's breath in yoga classes.

In the next chapter I turn to the art-making I have engaged in with Clementine over the last two years. Our time together could be described as a series of exercises in mindfulness as we experiment with making art together. It is at the same time a simple experiment in bringing the ideas I have been developing in this book into my own everyday practice, and documenting that as it plays out in our time spent painting together.

Note

1 Bandy is a very popular Swedish game, a little like ice-hockey, though the children's practice is on paved ground.

Chapter 5

The affective flows of art-making

I am always slightly surprised by what I do. That which acts through me is also surprised by what I do, by the chance to mutate, to change, and to bifurcate.

(Latour, 1999: 281)

Clementine and I have been drawing, painting, and story-making together since she was less than two years old. What we have each become through our art-making encounters, and what our art materials have become in their encounters with us, has continually taken me by surprise. As Deleuze and Guattari (1987: 257) say: "We know nothing about a body [a person, a paintbrush, a pencil, a tube of paint, a kitchen] until we know what it can do, in other words, what its affects are, how they can or cannot enter into composition with other affects, with the affects of another body".

Affects, in this Deleuzian sense, are surprising. They come from "the forces that pass between the parties, which provoke a change of state and create something new in them" (Deleuze, 1997: 127). The "parties" here, in our art-making, included Clementine and me, the art materials, the stories we created, and the communities and places we lived in. We were, in Barad's terms, a *"mutual constitution of entangled agencies"* (Barad, 2007: 33), affecting each other and being affected as we generated that "mood of enchantment or that strange combination of delight and disturbance" that emerges in the surprising unfolding of art-making (Bennett, 2010: xi).

The art materials that Clementine and I worked with as we made art together were not lifeless matter for us to manipulate in order to express our own individualized essence. Rather, as I will show here, the emergent processes of becoming-art-makers that we engaged in, unfolded themselves in intra-action with each other's emergent becoming, where those others included both human *and* non-human materialities, both ontologies *and* epistemologies.

Creating an art space

The first *drawing-story* with Clementine happened when she had just come back from a picnic with her cousins at Centennial Park. Claudia needed to do some shopping and asked me to mind her. Clementine climbed up on the seat opposite me in the café and I ordered her a baby-chino and a muffin. I asked her to tell me what she had done at the park. At eighteen months, the task of telling me a story of what they had done was just outside her reach. So I said, surprising myself, "Let's draw it." "Did you run?" I asked. "Yes," she said, so I quickly drew a stick-figure running, giving it curly hair and clothes like Clementine's, pointing out that the running figure had buttons on her dress the same as Clementine had on her dress. "Did you jump?" I asked. "Yes," she said, so I drew a picture of her jumping. "Not like that," she said, and climbed off her chair and showed me how she jumped. I rubbed out the first jumping figure and made it jump just as she'd shown me. The story grew through several pages to include each of her cousins, looking more or less recognizably themselves, playing together in the ways I offered and she assented to, and ways she told me or showed me. We created a story of climbing the magnificent old trees, and looking at the ducks on the lily pond. "The pond is scary," she said, staring at the duck pond I had drawn, waiting, it seemed, for its danger to be made evident by the quickly moving pencil. I attempted bland reassurances about the benign nature of the pond, which she didn't find at all convincing. So I took up the affect of danger and offered her a crocodile peeping its nose out of the water. She liked the crocodile and its possibilities very much. Would it bite her toes, we wondered . . . And so the story unfolded itself. I took the pages to my place and bound them together to make a book called *Clementine's Visit to Centennial Park*, and together we presented it to her delighted mother.

Some months later the idea of turning my kitchen into a place to paint seemed a natural extension of our story-making. To transform my kitchen into an art space meant giving up, to the extent that I could, the lines of descent of my quotidian kitchen-practices (a fastidious attention to cleanliness, order, and predictability), and opening myself up to the surprise of the new. Clementine, for her part, had to be able to forgive those small anxieties attached to order. Some months into our painting together I exclaimed "No!" as she was about to do something I didn't want her to do. She literally jumped in her seat and I realized with a shock how hard she worked at accommodating my ongoing quotidian lapses. Despite my passionate attachment to lines of ascent I find in my notes, two years after we had begun painting and drawing together, the following moment:

> Clementine dipped a pencil in the paint and made some dots. I said that wasn't what the pencils were for. She looked up at me, hesitating, and I realized what a stupid thing that was to say. So I said, "Sometimes adults have ideas that are wrong. Show me what you were doing". She showed how she could make small vivid dots using the pencil. I told her that was good, and that experimenting was good, and that sometimes I say things that are wrong, though often I am right as well. She seemed happy with that. She made some more dots, but then wanted to clean the paint off the pencil. I was appalled at myself.

Each time we got together to paint I covered the bench surfaces with newspaper so I wouldn't worry about where the paint landed, and we painted on recycled paper from my study to avert any unwanted anxieties I might have about waste, and so there wouldn't be any demand from the paper that only perfectly executed paintings could appear on it. Spillages of paint and water, or wet paintings that landed upside down on the floor, came to be defined by us as "accidents", over which there would be no drama. Clementine's paintings, when she was especially pleased with them, went up on the walls of her own apartment. Some of mine went up on my kitchen walls. What I sought in this new order, these lines of descent, was a space in which art could happen, where we could joyfully, and without any unnecessary anxieties, open up lines of ascent as we experimented with art-making.

The first time we decided to do painting, Clementine sat up at the kitchen bench, watching attentively as I put everything we would need in place. I put a sculpture of an exotic, blue bird on the bench as possible inspiration for our work. I asked Clementine to choose which colours she wanted and squeezed these out in generous dollops onto the small palette, each into its own small indentation, and we each chose a brush from among the many different sized and textured brushes. I showed her how to dip hers into the glass of water and then into the paint she wanted to work with. To my surprise she dipped the brush into all of the colours, one after the other, before beginning her painting. I felt a rush of anxiety about this instant "messing up" of colours, exclaiming "Oh!" and then watching in fascination as her brush dipped into one and now another of the vivid colours, resisting my resistance.

She began working with great speed, moving from one painting to the next, as far as I could see, ignoring the bird. I too got into the swing of moving rapidly, as I'd already learned to do in our drawing-stories, not worrying about how the "product" might turn out. With rapid brush strokes I found the bird appearing on my page in a way that delighted me, and that I had not imagined myself capable of. The legs of the bird in my painting were too short as the page wasn't long enough to extend them to the right length. Realizing the too-shortness didn't matter gave me intense pleasure as I found myself liberated from one of many small enslavements to how art *ought* to be. Letting the brush flow and the colours mix in unexpected ways was a skill I began picking up from Clementine right there in that first encounter. Together we listened to each other, as we became emergent-artists-together, open to being affected by each other and to what we might create. I was so delighted with my bird painting that it lived on the wall for some time next to the bird itself. On subsequent visits Clemmie would point with delight to the bird and then the painting, saying "See, bird, bird", as if surprised all over again by what had appeared on my page. (See Plate 1.)

At the end of each painting session I would move her chair over to the kitchen sink and we would wash ourselves and the art materials. Anticipating that there might be danger because the hot tap was in such easy reach, I personified each of the taps, giving a deep gravelly voice to the hot tap, which said, "Watch out! I'm the hot tap. I'm really dangerous!" and to the cold tap a mild soft voice that said, "Hello, I'm the cold tap. I don't hurt anyone." Clementine loved these voices and took great pleasure in repeating them. When it came time to let out the water, knowing that the drain might make a rather startling noise, I invented a funny gurgling voice for the plug-hole that talked nonsense to Clementine while it took away the water. As we cleaned up together I learned to notice the colour of the water as the paint washed out of the brushes, while she learned the nature of the different brushes and how to care for them. She learned how to be safe with the taps while I discovered a playful capacity to animate the taps and the plughole. Together with brushes and paint and water we entered a timeless zone of play where lines of ascent and descent worked together in harmony.

Moments of becoming art-makers

What follows are brief excerpts from the notes I made after each painting session. I have chosen out of more than 250 paintings and drawings moments that reveal the surprising nature of our art-making, and the intra-active, affective flows in between. I have chosen as well moments that show the tension between the lines of descent, always at work, and the contrasting liveliness and joy of mutual composition.

13 October 2011: Order supporting the flow of affect and the emergence of the new

Today was our first time painting together after me having been away for six weeks. When we left her place to come to my place, Scout cried as she wanted to come too, and Clementine, now 2 years and 10 months old, explained to her that painting was only for big girls.

When we arrived in my kitchen Clementine moved her chair over to the bench, saying, "This is my chair," and climbed up onto the chair, asking where the paints were. As usual I talked about the preparation as I got everything ready . . . I am fascinated by how quiet and how patient she is as she watches it all being laid out . . .

Today she had insisted that she bring her doll, Archer, and announced that she was going to paint Archer. She nodded toward my painting of the bird on the wall and said, "You painted that yesterday" (her word for any time past). Our painting together was rarely about *representing* a specific object such as the doll or the bird. If we worked with objects they were more like leaping-off points for whatever line of flight might emerge. Today she had chosen Archer, and so we sat him on the bench where we could see him. As I squeezed out the colours, we discussed how red and white together would make pink. She immediately mixed these colours and began her painting with playful sweeping lines. Then she moved to blue and white, and some gold, overlaying these on the pink.

Meanwhile I began with a pink circle for Archer's face and a pink smile. She glanced at it and said, "That's you." I accepted that I was not painting Archer but myself. We discussed what colour my hair should be and we decided on gold. I gave myself blue and gold eyes and a stick figure body.

Clementine engaged in more experimental mixing of colours and brush strokes, combining blue and pink, incorporating the circle I had begun my painting with. She moved from there to experimenting with combining blue and yellow to make green, using both circular and straight brush strokes.

Her free and confident brush strokes, layering one colour on top of another and mixing colours, and her idea that I was painting myself led to my own experiment. I was amazed at what emerged. A wild, angry, crazy-looking face. All the grief and anger I feel about my current work situation was suddenly visible on the page.

I was so surprised I held it up for Clementine to see and said, "Look at that!" She looked at it and exclaimed, "Oh! It's a really angry spider mother!" (See Plate 2.)

Her next two paintings incorporated some of the colours and lines of the spider-mother. She abandoned the brushes and began doing dots with paint on her fingers and then sliding her fingers through the paint. It was as if my wild painting gave her permission to do something outside the ordinary. She then began a new painting using the same colours with a brush, but this time picked up a pencil lying there and made squiggly lines in the paint that captured the affect of the angry spider mother. (See Plates 3 and 4.)

25 October 2011: Expanding the field of material engagements

[Clementine has been sick, so this was the first time painting together after a break. After we finished painting and cleaned up, we played with the dolls and then Clementine noticed for the first time my bowl of brightly coloured wool.]

She asked me could she do knitting. I said she would have to be bigger before she could do knitting. She did not find this at all convincing. I showed her how knitting is done and she accepted it might be too hard. She began cutting pieces of black wool into odd-sized strips, taking pleasure in the fact that she could use the scissors so well. She looked at all the rest of the wool and seemed to think cutting it all up would be fun, starting in on a ball of green wool and cutting through the whole ball. I said gently that I hadn't really wanted her to do that, and began an alternative game that we would make a spider from the black bits of wool she had cut. I rapidly made two spiders with red eyes and she thought they were scary and wonderful. We played with those for a while and then she said she wanted to write on the computer. So she sat on my knee and typed the first few words, with me telling her how to spell them, and pointing to the relevant keys. She then dictated for me to type:

> Dear clemmie
> I hope you are alright.
> Dear scoutie
> I hope you are alright.
> Dear mummy
> I hope you are alright.
> Dear grandma
> I hope you are alright.
> Get well soon
> We all go to bed last night and
> We had sweet dreams

She was aware that the words on the screen were the words she was saying to me, pointing to the words and repeating what she had said. When I said we had left Daddy out, she said no, he couldn't be there as he hadn't been sick. She hadn't been sure how to end her poem, and so I had suggested the sweet dreams, which she accepted with a smile.

27 February 2012: Joyfully entering into composition together

Today began in the coffee shop. In this storytelling Clementine told the story and I drew it. She began with herself and Scout, and her cousins, and their parents, each with a mermaid tail. Each of the mermaids had spots on their faces, which Clemmie added, at first with pencil and then, realizing we have one, with red pen. The red spots grew into wild scribbles, which could be cuts. The spots meant that everyone was sick and had to be rushed to hospital. I drew an ambulance rushing along to take them to the hospital. We only had one page, so we had to go across to the newsagent for more, as she was determined the story would continue. (See Plate 5.)

There are seven beds for the mermaids to lie in, and a doctor with some pills for them, some big double doors to go through. The new baby-to-be, Sunday, is now included, with a bed of his own, and Clemmie has two beds, one for her when she is three, as she currently is, and one when she is a very big girl. Everyone takes their pills. I draw the pills in their tummies. The two Clementines had to have an especially big pill. When they were well, I added a sports car for Clemmie to drive off in, and I drew her hair whooshing behind her in the wind. She coloured in the car with the red pen. (See Plate 6.)

Now the story moves to the park. She loves this part of the story where her toes are bitten by a crocodile. This has many variations. Today the park had a tree and a ladder and a slippery dip – a long slippery dip at the end of which one could fly down into the boat on the water. Clementine climbed the ladder and went "whoosh" down the slippery dip with her hair flying and landed on the boat. Then she dived into the water, knowing the crocodile would be there. She insisted her arms were not going over her head in a crawl, but in front of her in a dog paddle. So I changed the arms to dog paddle arms. The crocodile nipped her mermaid tail. She swam fast toward her mum, calling, "Mum! Mum!" who was also in the water. I suggested a bandaid for the nip in her tail, and that made it better. On the next page, the mermaids have gone to an ice-skating rink where two mermaids, covered in bandaids, go skating. In the top left-hand corner, in red, is Clementine's drawing of hair flying out behind. (See Plates 7 and 8.)

28 February 2012: A surprising leap into something new – hair blowing in the wind

Next day, Clemmie is very keen to come to my place to paint, even though I warn her we have only half an hour. She begins with a pink fish and some water and the wind blowing. Next she paints herself with hair blowing wildly in the wind and then Scout with hair blowing wildly in the wind. In each case the blowing hair takes up most of the page and is full of colour and movement. (See Plates 9 and 10.)

What was magical for me in these sessions was to see the way that our story from the day before leapt over into her paintings with the fish, and the hair blowing in the wind. And much bigger than that really is the way she drew on all the skills she has been developing in experimenting with brushes and colour and lines. It was an amazing day.

23 May 2012: Drawing stories together as joyful composition

[After several paintings] Clementine chose the calligraphy brush and began with dots in the corners representing her house and her friends' houses. Then she drew flowing lines back and forth between the houses, some with mud puddles. She called it Clemmie's house, and all her friends' houses, and visiting friends and adventures with crocodiles. As she painted she told the story of a very brave girl in her painting called Clementine who was the bravest mermaid. Her friends were all there. There were so many crocodiles chasing them and they couldn't run fast enough and the crocodiles were biting them and they had to go to hospital. (See Plate 11.)

At that point she stopped and asked could we draw a mermaid story. I said she could draw but she was adamant that I should draw because I am "so good at it" and she would sit on my knee, she said, and we would tell the story together. We drew two mermaids, Jazzie and Clemmie. Clemmie was the biggest mermaid. The hands of the mermaids had to look like Clemmie's

hands, not the stick fingers I had quickly drawn. (Recently we have been tracing around our fingers and painting them so she has an image of how fingers
should be.) Jazzie had a cut in her tail. Clemmie and Jazzie both had thorns in
their tails and had to go to hospital. They were each in a hospital bed and very
sad. Dr Bronny came with her bandaids and tweezers, and the sad faces turned
into smiles. Dr Bronny pulled out the thorns and put them in a bowl and put a
bandaid on Jazzie's cut. I said they said "Ouch!" when the thorns were pulled
out, but they didn't say "Ouch", she said, and she didn't want their words written, so I rubbed them out. Then she noticed that mermaid Scout and mermaid
Maxie were hiding under the beds . . . All during the storytelling and drawing she squirmed with excitement, almost squirming off my lap several times.
I wouldn't have known the level of excitement in our drawing stories if she
hadn't been on my lap!

This was one of the most creative and relaxed sessions we have had for a
while, and one where the love between us has been palpable.

25 June 2012: The emergence of thought about our collective materiality

This was a most relaxed and joyful session with Clementine – though they are
always that, this time together seemed qualitatively different. When we met
by chance on the front stairs she jumped up into my arms and hugged me and
asked if she could come to my place. She said she had missed me so much while
I was away though I had only been gone for five days . . . She reminds me the
baby is due in three weeks.

When we got to my place she was hungry and asked me to cut up a pear. We
talked about how pears and people were alike. The pear had skin like her, and a
round tummy like her mummy. She said she had a round tummy too. We then
wondered about the seeds and whether she had seeds, but she thought not. I
jokingly asked her if she had a stalk sprouting out of her head and she laughed
and said no. I asked if she wanted toast, with butter and honey, and she said
yes, but she would also like on her toast some of my little red seeds with white
fingers. It took me a while to work out that she meant pomegranate seeds, so I
cut open the pomegranate and she showed me the little white fingers on each
seed, which she said were not good to eat, and I agreed. We wondered how
pomegranates and people were alike and decided the red juice in the pomegranate was like blood. She observed that in people it was better for the blood
to stay inside and not come outside the body.

Finally we got round to painting. She drew some fluffy clouds, telling me
she was good at clouds, and indeed she was. She painted them pink, mixing
white and red, and told me they were awesome pink clouds. She thoroughly
mixed all the colours I had put on the palette, and the resulting muddy paint
on her brush then rather spoiled the clouds. I suggested brown was not great
for clouds and she stopped, leaving some of the pink still visible. Curiously she

named her painting *pitta patta rainbow*, and when I asked wasn't it called clouds she said no. So I have not yet got a clue as to what she is doing with the naming. (See Plate 12).

She said she didn't want to do any more painting, so while I finished my painting she drew a picture of her mummy's tummy with the baby in. She then painted over the drawing, became upset and wanted to rub the paint off. She was rubbing a hole in the paper and I suggested she stop before she had a hole. She stopped, but then produced two new watery paintings, which she rubbed a hole in. She didn't seem upset when she did this – just very intent on rubbing until she got a hole. She asked me to draw Claudia with the baby coming out with Clementine beside her looking sad as she had the hiccups. She insisted that the baby was a girl, though she knows the baby coming is a boy. Next drawing was the whole family, with the baby still in Mummy's tummy, and Scout with a baby in her tummy (just pretending, she said, it's really Archer, the doll). (See Plates 13 and 14.)

23 July 2012: Attending to the small details of the flow between us two, the poppies and the bees

I have Clementine to visit for a few hours. Claudia's baby is due any day.

When I showed Clemmie my vase of poppies as our inspiration for painting she asked me did I know that flowers need water and sun and earth to grow. Right then a poppy flower unfolded from its pod and we talked about how it was like a butterfly unfolding its wings from the cocoon that the caterpillar has made. Over lunch we talked about the lettuce seedlings she and I planted in the community garden, and the fact that they are growing, and she said we should get some seeds from the poppy and plant them. I said that the flower needed bees to pollinate them and there are no bees inside the apartment, so there will be no seeds. She told me that bees make honey, and I got out the honey jar and she showed me the picture of the bee on the lid. "See, bee-honey, bee-honey. See?" she said, pointing to the picture of the bee and the actual honey in turn, showing me how obvious the connection was. We looked in detail at the beautiful yellow centre of the flowers and talked about how bees pollinate flowers. I told her about the little sacs some bees have on their legs to carry the pollen, and about how the flower relies on the bees to put the pollen down the small space in the middle of the flower to begin the process of making seeds. And how the flower, if the bee pollinates it, will turn into seeds that we could plant and make more poppies. We had some toast and honey to get the feel of bees and honey and poppies and how amazing the bees really are. Then we did paintings of poppies and Clemmie wrote a poem to go with each of the paintings. The "pitta patta" title of her paintings that puzzled me so much for the repetitiveness and apparent lack of meaning relating to the painting has finally budded into a poem that is a little like an ode to a bee and butterfly combined:

Pitta patta
catty pillar
Pitty pea . . .
I want you
To be my bee.

Today I wanted to paint the poppies . . . I asked Clemmie to leave my green paint green, and my orange orange, as they were the colours I needed, but she couldn't resist mixing them to see what would happen, and once again the mixes were better than I would have done for myself, adding (somewhat random) depth and variation, whereas I would have happily stayed (boringly and uninspired) with mono colours. When Clemmie flicked drops of wet paint onto my painting I was a little upset. I said, "Oh, I didn't want that," using a tissue to soak up the splodges of water. She looked quite puzzled, not knowing why I might not want those random flicks of colour. She teased me (with a little smile) by using her paint-loaded brush to show me where on my painting I might put some stars (there were some star stickers I had put in the paint box). When I objected quite firmly, she smiled and turned her brush around and showed me with the handle end where I might put the stars. When I said I didn't want stars she accepted that and continued with her own glorious painting of poppies. (See Plates 15 and 16.)

(In)conclusion

Sitting across the kitchen bench from each other, creating an art-making-space together, Clementine and I experience a peculiar attentiveness to each other's drawing and painting that is evident in the elements of our paintings and drawings that jump from her page to mine, and mine to hers; her excitement infects me just as my pleasure in our quiet play with pencils and paints infects her. Together we have responded to the spaces we have created by developing a joyful engagement in the practice of drawing and painting together. The speed with which she painted enabled me to let go of an idea that painting involved slow and painstaking attention to representation. Her mixing of colours gave me the possibility of lines of flight that did not emerge from a carefully laid down plan or knowledge of colours. I see, too, as I look through the 250 paintings so far, that she returns again and again to the story of the flight to hospital, and I have not mentioned in my notes that she had had first-hand experience of such a flight when she severed her finger in a sliding door.

There was much that happened outside our art-making – my grief at my work situation, or my visit to an inspiring exhibition of paintings of flowers by the Japanese artist Secca. There were many other forces at play that, of necessity, I cannot be aware of. I notice too that I have not found space to document here the generous and warm encouragement that Clementine's parents, Matt and Claudia, gave to our art-making. Claudia's delight in the paintings and drawings and stories Clementine brought home were vital to our work; their filming of some of our times together, their willingness to put her paintings up on their walls . . . all of this was integral to the community that made our art-making possible – not to mention the forbearance of the workers in the coffee shop who dealt with spilt baby-chinos, crumbled muffins, and pencils and papers everywhere. I'd like to think I've exaggerated my adherence to quotidian, repetitive lines of descent, but the surprise and exhilaration I felt at being freed from them cannot be made real unless I admit the extent that they were there, constraining what it was possible for me to do. Being open to that sense of surprise and joy in the affective flow of our art-making is what I have most gained from our work together. I have learned through this work together to listen differently, to be open with all my senses to what is unexpected and new, and to be affected by it. Like Halsey swimming in his ocean wave, we created together moments of *haecceity* or grace when, immersed in the affective flows between ourselves and the paint, the brushes, and the pencils, we were no longer separate entities – no longer beings limited to what we already knew:

> A haecceity is a moment of pure speed and intensity (an *individuation*) – like when a swimming body becomes-wave and is momentarily suspended in nothing but an intensity of forces and rhythms. Or like when body becomes-horizon such that it feels only the interplay between curves and surfaces and knows nothing of here and there, observer and observed.
>
> (Halsey, 2007: 146)

In the next and final chapter I explore another experiment with bringing the ideas in this book into my everyday practice. It involved me in re-writing one of my favourite stories from childhood. Originally written in 1945, the story had been re-written in 1974 and turned into the worst kind of moralistic tale. My rewriting of the story (O'Harris, 2014) takes it on another trajectory. It decomposes the 1974 moralistic tale and sets out to create characters with the power to change Fairyland through their intra-active becomings with each other, and who enable Fairyland to expand its capacity for thought and for being.

Chapter 6

Lines of flight in stories for children

Arriving now at the final chapter of this book, I want to explore through writing stories for children the implications of what has unfolded in each of the previous chapters. I open up a diffractive space of thought about writing stories for children based on my own experience of re-writing the Australian children's classic *The Fairy Who Wouldn't Fly* (O'Harris, 2014). Deleuze and Guattari invited us, in 1987, to think about and to write books differently. They suggested that, rather than basing our stories on individualized enunciations, with subjects trapped in dominant modes of subjectification and patterns of desire, we generate books as *assemblages*:

> An assemblage, in its multiplicity, necessarily acts on semiotic flows, material flows, and social flows simultaneously . . . There is no longer a tripartite division between a field of reality (the world) and a field of representation (the book) and a field of subjectivity (the author) . . . there is a collective assemblage of enunciation, a machinic assemblage of desire, one inside the other and both plugged into an immense outside that is a multiplicity in any case.
>
> (Deleuze and Guattari, 1987: 23)

Such a book, they suggest, does not merely trace over that which already exists, "an endless tracing of established concepts and words, a tracing of the world present, past, and future" (Deleuze and Guattari, 1987: 24). The book they envisage involves, as well, a nomadic mapping. Such a book is concerned with multiplying possibilities, with movement rather than stasis. It de-territorializes apparently fixed cultural lines, and the de-territorialized spaces those lines created will be re-territorialized in a constant movement. Lines of ascent and descent are always intermingling, always affecting each other: "[T]here is a *mutual immanence* of the lines. And it is not easy to sort them out. No one of them is transcendent, each is at work within the others" (205).

My challenge, then, was to write a story about mutual becoming, a story that de-territorialized the dominant modes of enunciation and patterns of desire. I wanted a book that would work at this interface between striations and emergent becomings. I wanted characters who could take up Deleuzian lines-of-flight.

The Fairy Who Wouldn't Fly was written and illustrated by Pixie O'Harris in 1945, and re-written 30 years later by David Harris, with new illustrations by Pixie O'Harris. When I was a child I read and re-read the '45 version. The nickname my father gave me was Fairy. The '74 version, however, written when my children were beginning to read, was entirely different. In both versions the narrative trajectory is from unacceptable individual difference to normality. But the processes through which normalization is accomplished differ radically (Davies, 2005). What remains the same in '45 and '74 is that the Fairy-who-wouldn't-fly, and all the other creatures who won't do as they should, are banished from Fairyland and sent to the *Woodn't*. There they must stay until they learn to conform to (or are re-territorialized within) the specific categorizations and striations (that is, the rigid structures and organization) of Fairyland.

The story, in both versions, is a moralistic tale; that is, it assumes there is a correct way to be, an idealized form that each being must always aspire to. The ideal form lies outside each of them, and their task is to incorporate it within their individualized, separate beings (Deleuze, 1980). In 1945, however, the Fairy is both lovable and rebellious, struggling within and against the attempts to re-territorialize or normalize her. In '74 the Fairy is pathologized; she longs to be the same as other fairies but is overwhelmed by her fear of failure. In both '45 and '74 the category of "fairy" requires the one so categorized to be busy and useful, and to use her wings to fly.

In 1945 there is a loving but authoritarian structure against which the Fairy rebels. She is expelled from Fairyland and sent to the Woodn't. Her intra-actions there with other rebels lead to a joyful discovery of flight and her subsequent return to Fairyland. In '45 the elves explained to the Fairy when they dropped her off in the Woodn't that she could only come home to Fairyland when she learnt to fly as the other fairies did. The striations were thus made clear, but so was love for the Fairy. The Fairy's resistance to flight was not pathologized, even if it was not, in the final event, to be accepted. When the elves explained why the Fairy Queen had banished her she was very angry. In 1974, in marked contrast, the Fairy did not ask for an explanation for her banishment, and was not offered one. She assumed that she could and must find out for herself the *reasons* why the Queen had sent her to the Woodn't. She took for granted that the banishment was a cure for her pathological condition, which she must strive to overcome. The moral of the '74 story: everyone must strive to overcome those limitations that prevent them from becoming what their categorizations say they must be. No exceptions. In 1945 the Fairy's resistance to flying was construed in terms of an endearing childish playfulness and the possibility that she had been too indulged as a baby. In '74 the Fairy has become self-conscious, a faulty ego, with her judgemental gaze turned in on herself.

In my experimental re-mapping of the story I introduce a quite different narrative trajectory; not one of opposition or resistance to the forces of normalization, and certainly not one of individualized pathology. I wanted a story that moved *in-between*, on the one hand, the forces that would hold everything the same, placing everything within already-known categories, and on the other, the lines of force and the encounters that might open up the not-yet-known. My story would work at the interface of lines of ascent and descent. A line of ascent is made up of multiple small flights, and it ruptures rigid lines and stratifications. It enters into a diffractive relationship or entangled enlivening of being *with* the lines of descent and their tendency to hold everything the same.

In Bergson's philosophy, as in Deleuze and Guattari's and in Barad's, no being can exist in isolation. Each is always affected by the other beings with which it is entangled – not just human beings, but non-human beings, both organic and inorganic. What comes to matter, and what matter comes to be, is always emergent in the movement in-between intra-active becomings. I wanted my story to actively engage with matter and with the ways things are made to matter.

I wanted a book that worked at these multiple interfaces, that engaged in this movement in-between; not a book that rejects the striations, but a book that explores the diffraction of forces that territorialize, and re-territorialize through endless repetitions of the already known, and the emergent possibilities of de-territorialization. At the same time I wanted it to pose a challenge to thinking-as-usual. I wanted to create adults who might listen to children; I wanted creatures who were open to encounters with the material world in ways that affected them. That meant creating creatures who not only listened to each other, but who might listen to, and be affected by, the vitality of non-human others. A leaf fluttering on the breeze. A road. A tree. A storm. I wanted creatures who could de-territorialize dominant modes of enunciation. I wanted normative lines of force vulnerable to those de-territorializing movements. I wanted a book that drew the reader into the act of listening, with all their senses, to the minute details of life in its specificity and emergent multiplicities. I wanted an aesthetic book, an ethical book, a book that entered into what Barad (2007) calls an *ethico-onto-epistem-ology*, working with and between vibrant matter, modes of enunciation, and ethics. Not world, book, and author separate, but mutually entangled in the enlivening of being. Not just cognitive and didactic, but resonating, capable of affecting the reader.

I wanted a book that did not impose a morally ascendant viewpoint, and did not develop its meanings in opposition or in resistance to the forces of normalization. I wanted to map out a life form that creatively evolves (through opposing but inseparable lines of ascent and descent), not through the single-minded imposition of categories or moralisms, and not through the body realizing its essential nature, but through a celebration of multiplicity and difference emergent in the ongoing intra-actions between meaning and matter, where each affects the other, and where each moment matters (Barad, 2007).

At the same time I wanted emergent meanings that intra-acted with the materiality of the characters and their specificity. I wanted my re-written story to explore what happens when something comes to matter, and when it actively changes the way things are and are perceived to be. I wanted what matter comes to be, and how meanings come to matter, to remain an open question (Barad, 2007). I wanted to de-territorialize categories and their power to limit thought and action.

My 2014 Fairy resists the pressure to be like other fairies, not because she is spoilt, or afraid, but because she is engaged in emergent listening, with all her senses:

> The Fairy-who-wouldn't-fly loved to lie about all day in her hammock amid the swaying blossoms. She listened to the wind and watched the clouds sailing high overhead. She watched the bees gathering honey, and the birds sipping nectar from the flowers. When she folded her wings and closed her eyes, she looked just like a dried leaf, so no one could see her.
>
> The other fairies, their bright, beautiful wings flashing in the sunlight, worked hard in the bush. They lifted up the heads of flowers after rain, helped lame beetles over bush tracks, and saved silly baby birds, who fell out of their nests before they were ready to fly. They helped to keep the bushland and all its creatures healthy and strong.
>
> But the Fairy-who-wouldn't-fly was not the same as other fairies. Instead of working, she wanted to read, to sleep, and to dream. And when she woke, she would wonder about things. She wondered where the wind came from, and she wondered how seeds knew what kind of flower to grow into. She wondered about her friend the Leaf-cutter Bee, who made delicious pollen cupcakes. She hadn't seen her for such a long time.

The Leaf-cutter Bee appears for the first time in 2014. She has been banished for not being like the honey-bees and living in a hive. Leaf-cutter bees are native Australian bees who do not actually live in hives. (See Plate 17.[1]) She has been banished through the imposition of a category in just the way Bergson is so scathing about in scientific practice:

> Our reason, incorrigibly presumptuous, imagines itself possessed . . . of all the essential elements of the knowledge of truth. Even where it confesses that it does not know the object presented to it, it believes that its ignorance consists only in not knowing which one of its time-honoured categories suits the new object.
>
> (Bergson, 1998: 48)

The Bee will play an important role, particularly in the story's ending.

When the Fairy arrives in the Woodn't, the Frog-who-wouldn't-hop welcomes her and introduces her to all the other creatures who won't do what they should. As night falls they make their way home to the cave where they live together.

> "Where are we to sleep?" asked the Fairy.
> "On the floor, I'm afraid," said the Bee.
> "Are there no cobweb hammocks?"
> The Glow-worm laughed a queer little laugh. "No," she said. "There has only been one spider in the Woodn't and that was the Spider-who-wouldn't-spin."
> The Fairy felt hot tears stinging her eyes. She had never slept on a hard dirt floor before.
> "I'm growing tired of all these creatures who won't do things," she said crossly.
> "Must be tired of yourself then, Miss," said the Glow-worm.
> "Don't be rude. Go to sleep," interrupted the Frog.
> "I want to sleep in the middle," said the Bat, pushing the Fairy.
> "Move over," said the Bee. "You're crowding me!"
> "You can all have your stuffy cave! I'm going outside," said the Fairy. "Anything is better than being in here!"
> "Don't make me laugh," said the Kookaburra.
> "You couldn't, even if you tried," snapped the Fairy.
> *Oh no*, she thought as she walked out of the cave. *I'm becoming as grumpy as they are.*
> As she stood in the opening of the cave, she saw a huge full moon peeping up through the trees, yellow and glowing. The Flower was calling out, "Come and talk to me, dearie. Tell me all about yourself, I wish I could fly . . ."
> But the Fairy took a deep breath of cool air, and bravely walked out into the Woodn't.

While in '74 the Fairy is waylaid by the Flower (who won't go to sleep at night) and subjected to a patronizing lecture about the Fairy not knowing whether she can fly until she tries, the 2014 Fairy enters intra-actively into an encounter with the Woodn't, listening to it with all her senses, just as she had listened to the forest in Fairyland:

> The trees shone green and orange in the moonlight. They were really quite beautiful.
> "Hello trees," she said. "You're different, just like me, aren't you? Are you sad, too?"
> The tree trunks were smooth and glowing and they stretched their arms out toward her to comfort her. She heard the softest sigh coming from the treetops. She looked up, and in the bright moonlight she saw their leaves swaying gently in the breeze. Whishh!

What do I wish? she wondered. She wished for Fairyland, but she didn't wish to be like everyone else.

But . . . I wonder, thought the Fairy, *what it would be like to fly?* At that moment a leaf let go from the tree and fluttered slowly on the breeze, twirling down to the ground.

Through this emergent listening, the Fairy opens up a new encounter with her wings, not unlike the loving kindness that Anh showed toward his anger in the buddhist-inspired story in Chapter 4. The self she had previously rejected – a flying self – becomes someone she can also become:

The Fairy looked back at her wings. *I wonder if I can open them?*

She tried. It was hard at first, but at last, with a great effort, she was able to open them out wide.

"Oh!" she cried. "How amazing they are!"

With the moonlight shining on them they glittered, blue and green and red and yellow. Just like the lights in Fairyland.

When she moved her shoulders she found that she could make her wings flutter. "I wonder," she said. "I wonder if I *could* fly? What would it be like?"

She tried.

But it was not easy for wings that had not been used, and she didn't know the right way to begin.

Nearby was a jagged purple rock that reached high into the sky. She began to climb, and the sharp rock hurt her delicate fingers and toes. When she reached the top she looked down at the earth far beneath her. It seemed a long way away.

She could hear the trees sighing and the distant crickets singing. She stood still on the top of the rock and felt the breeze blowing gently against her wings.

Taking a deep breath, she jumped. At first she felt herself falling, but the breeze gently picked her up, and her wings began to open and shut *as if they knew the way to fly* all the time.

The Fairy floated like a piece of thistledown on to the grass.

First she laughed and then she cried, and then she jumped up and danced leaping into the air, then she talked to her wings and stroked them, telling them how beautiful they were, then she tried flying upward from the ground so often that she was quite worn out. It must have been a pretty sight. Her eyes were bright and her fairy heart was singing. At last she was so tired she fell fast asleep lying across the top of a toadstool, her lovely wings still quivering.

When she woke she felt so happy, not a bit like the grumpy Fairy who'd stormed out of the cave last night. She washed her hands and face in the dew, shook her lovely wings wide in the sunlight, singing with delight.

The Fairy's emergent multiplicity enables her to bravely and then joyfully take up flight, not in subservience to her categorization, or out of a need to de-pathologize herself, but as creative evolution of life's possibilities in intra-action with others.

In the Woodn't, after she wakes, she finds a small, lost mortal boy. The Fairy, with all the others, invents ways to take care of him. In the process the Frog begins to hop, the Kookaburra to laugh, and the Glow-worm to glow. When a storm comes they take the boy to the cave, where he falls asleep, along with the Flower, as he listens to the Fairy's beautiful song.

The Fairy and the Kookaburra fly up high into the sky to see if they can see the boy's home. (See Plate 18.) Together they get the lost boy home. The Kookaburra and the Frog go back to Fairyland to tell the Queen what has happened. The Queen is overjoyed and sends a beautiful carriage drawn by butterflies to bring the Fairy and her friends home. The carriage is driven by an elf with a funny cheery smile:

> "The Fairy Queen has sent her special carriage for you," he said, bowing to the Fairy. "The Frog and the Kookaburra arrived safely and told her how you saved the lost boy, and she wants you to return to Fairyland for ever."
>
> "How wonderful, how happy I will be," said the Fairy, with a big sigh. "Come on Bat, and Glowy and Flower. Are you coming, dear Bee?"
>
> "No, I don't think so," said the Bee. "I want to explore new places, and I want to find out what's killing the honey bees. I need to live on my own for a while and have time to think. Goodbye, dear Fairy, and Batty, and Flower and dear Glow-worm."
>
> With that, she flew off into the sky, away from the Woodn't and away from Fairyland.
>
> Into the soft blue carriage stepped the Fairy clinging tightly to the Flower with one hand and the Bat with the other while the Glow-worm sat in her hair.
>
> The elf called to the butterflies, they fluttered their lovely wings, the carriage rose into the air, and off they flew. They arrived in Fairyland just as the red sun was sinking into the west. Oh, the laughter and the joy!
>
> The other fairies ran to meet them and everyone hugged and kissed the Fairy and each other, and they all admired the Fairy's wings.
>
> The Flower settled her roots into the earth, folded her petals, and said firmly, "I'm a little tired – I think I'll take a nap," and in no time was fast asleep.
>
> The Fairy said she would like to thank the Queen, so she, the Glow-worm and the Bat were taken before her.
>
> The Bat whispered to the Fairy as they knelt there, and so did the Glow-worm, so the Fairy said bravely: "Dear Queen, this little Bat is still afraid to fly by night, would you please make him into a mouse. He says he

will be ever so good and run all your messages. And the Glow-worm says if you allow her to sit on the back of your throne she will shine for ever and ever."

The Queen smiled and waved her wand, and there beside the Fairy was a mouse with quivering whiskers all ready to run messages, and on the tip of her wand was the brightest glow-worm ever seen.

"Oh, thank you," cried the Fairy. "And what about the Frog and the Kookaburra, dear Queen?" she asked.

"They are here," said the Queen. "Their return has not been at all what I expected. The Kookaburra has asked that he be allowed to laugh only when it is about to rain, and I have given him the new title of Rain Herald. This is a surprising change, and I welcome it.

"The Frog has asked for the new name of Tree Frog, and because of his great kindness I have asked him to be the Caretaker of Lost Creatures."

"That is wonderful! They will be so happy!" the Fairy said. "But I'm afraid the Bee has chosen not to come back. She didn't want to live in a hive because she prefers to live outside. She has gone off on another adventure to find out what's ailing the honey bees. She sends you her very best wishes."

The Fairy Queen smiled at the Fairy. She was so brave and honest. "It's very hard to tell a Queen that she's been wrong, and I thank you for it. The Bee will be most welcome in Fairyland when she completes her investigation."

The Fairy's heart filled with joy when she heard the Queen's kind words.

"And what about you?" asked the Queen. "Is there nothing you want for yourself?"

"I would like to change my name," said the Fairy shyly.

The Queen waved her bright wand over the Fairy's head and said softly, "Welcome Fairy Fleet-Wing."

"Dear Queen," said Fairy Fleet-Wing, "I would like to ask one more favour. Can I find the Bee and help her search for the answer to the honey bees' sickness. I believe that Fairyland and all the wide world depends on the bees. I would like to find out how to help them."

The Fairy Queen felt a large teardrop falling from her eye. She would miss this brave Fairy so much.

"My best wishes go with you Fairy Fleet-Wing," she said. "Good luck!"

She waved her wand over the Fairy and one hundred magic stars flowed down into the Fairy's hands.

In this new narrative the primacy of self-as-identity, characterized by individualism, competition, vulnerability, fear, and conformity, gives way to creative evolution, which emerges from the diffractive meetings, the mutually agentic entanglement, of meanings, matter, and ethics. The ethics of my story gives primacy to movement, to the eruption of the new, while at the same time not letting go of the fact that any new idea must not come into existence at the expense of other beings, and without letting go of a commitment to the multiplicity of truths as a value (Badiou, 2001). At the same time, it commits the necessary offence of rupturing those elements of the thinking-as-usual that are limiting or damaging, and that withhold a viable life from some to the benefit of others. The 2014 story gives primacy to diffractive movement over stasis, and to ~~subjects~~, collectively, generating new modes of being. It is interested in opening up as yet un-thought possibilities where ideas and the beings who experience those ideas are open to change. It seeks "to expose and make sense of the potential for radical innovation (revolution, invention, transfiguration . . .) in every situation" (Hallward, 2002: viii). As such, it unfolds a commitment to encounters, to emergent listening, and to intra-active becoming in which one does not come to exist independent of, or prior to, the moment of encounter – but over and over again within each moment. As Deleuze and Guattari say:

> To think is to experiment, but experimentation is always that which is in the process of coming about – the new, remarkable, and interesting that replace the appearance of truth and are more demanding than it is.
>
> (1994: 111)

(In)conclusion

And so, finally, I must bring to a close this assemblage of stories and concepts, in which I have opened up thought about, and affect in relation to, listening to children. I have engaged you in encounters with children, and asked you to be open to being affected by them. I have talked about encounters, here, as able to make us more fully alive in the world, and more joyful, or, alternatively, as able to deprive us of power, leading to sadness, to impotence, and a reduction in our ability to act. I have offered an ethics that gives preference to the former, and which affirms life and its capacity for action and for differentiation. I have suggested that we can learn from children about such an ethics, and about joyful encounters, if only we know how to listen to them.

As you have made your way through this book I have, in one way and another, asked you to listen to children, and to listen to thought unfolding. I have challenged you with the idea that listening is about not being bound by what you already know, even while new thought and emergent listening depends on the striations of that already-known world. I have invited you to think about life as movement, as a process of differentiation where becoming different is not understood in terms of its opposition to sameness, but as life itself.

Through each of the chapters I have asked you not to think, as we usually do, in dualistic terms, where something is always classified as this *or* that. I have invited you into a world that is not divided into binary structural oppositions

– subject *or* object, individual *or* collective, one *or* many, same *or* different, conservative *or* radical, thought *or* action, rational *or* emotional. Rather, I have offered, in place of structure, life itself in motion. To think in this way is to think in terms of AND rather than OR:

> AND is neither one thing nor the other, it's always in between, between two things; it's the borderline, there's always a border, a line of flight or flow, only we don't see it, because it's the least perceptible of things. And yet it's along this line of flight that things come to pass, becomings evolve, revolutions take shape.
>
> (Deleuze, 1995: 45)

A boy and a book; two boys, a girl, and a rock face; a boy and sand; a girl and sand and water; two boys and a song; a child, an adult, and paint; a fairy discovering flight and a leaf fluttering on the breeze . . .

I have asked you to think of the children, not as other to yourself, and not even as small people you might develop a heightened awareness of, but of the children *and* yourselves. Through expanding thought, and through focusing on the specificity of being, I have set out to enliven your imagination, and to mobilize affect and intuition. In this way I have invited you to enter into encounters with children, in which you are open to being affected by what you hear, and by the affect flowing between you, where each self, your own and the child's, "is a threshold, a door, a becoming between two" (Deleuze and Guattari, 1987: 249).

Through stories that capture the specificity of individual children, I have sought to open up the idea that the very specificity of each individual is *mobile* and *intra-active*. I have argued that our capacity to enter into encounters, to re-compose and decompose ourselves, our capacity to be affected, *enhances* that specificity and expands our capacity for thought and for action. Being open, and being vulnerable to being affected by the other, is how we accomplish our humanity; it is how the communities, of which we are part, create and re-create themselves. We are not separate from the encounters that make up our communities but, rather, I have suggested, we are emergent with them.

The thinking in this book has been deeply affected by the Reggio Emilia philosophy, which advocates listening to children as a significant part of its philosophy and practice. Being open to difference and to new thought is integral to the kind of listening that Reggio Emilia philosophy advocates. It requires practitioners capable of thinking creatively about what they are doing with children. It is a philosophy that is impacting on early childhood research and education everywhere, asking of researcher-practitioners that they work with concepts to open up new ways of seeing and being in their work with children.

Undermining this flowering of thought, and the evolution of new ideas, is neoliberalism, which devotes itself, in the formation of education policies, to the production of generic individuals whose function is to make a contribution to the market economy. Neoliberalism's focus is regulatory and based on the micro-management of the production of measurable and uniform outcomes. Reggio Emilia philosophy, in contrast, values difference, creativity, relationality, and the emergence of new thought. All of these are vital to the well-being of specific individuals and their communities.

It is demanding work to translate philosophical concepts into practice, and what I have sought to do here is to show how that might be done. I have sought, through stories of encounters with children, to bring a number of concepts vividly to life, showing their power to open up new ways of thinking and of intra-acting with children, new ways of valuing children and of learning with them how to engage in ethical practice, which asks in each moment what is being made to matter, and with what effect. It is an ethical and responsible philosophy that has at its heart the desire to listen to the other and to value emergent differences as integral to life itself.

Note

1 This drawing of the Leaf-cutter Bee (Plate 17), and the next of the Fairy and the Kookaburra (Plate 18), were created by Dan Davies for the new edition. They were, however, rejected by the estate owners, and so couldn't be included in the 2014 version of the book.

References

Badiou, A. (2000) *Deleuze: The clamor of being* (trans. L. Burchill). Minneapolis, MN: University of Minnesota Press.

Badiou, A. (2001) *Ethics: An essay on the understanding of evil* (trans. P. Hallward). New York: Verso Press.

Badiou, A. (2008) *Conditions* (trans. S. Corcoran). London: Continuum.

Barad, K. (2007) *Meeting the Universe Halfway: Quantum physics and the entanglement of matter and meaning*. Durham, NC: Duke University Press.

Bennett, J. (2010) *Vibrant Matter*. Durham, NC: Duke University Press.

Bergson, H. (1998) *Creative Evolution*. Mineola, NY: Dover Publications Inc.

Berlant, L. (2010) "Cruel optimism". In M. Gregg and G. J. Seigworth (eds), *The Affect Theory Reader*. London: Duke University Press, pp. 93–117.

Bradshaw, J. (2009) "Mirror neurons and empathy for pain". *Ockham's Razor*. ABC Radio. 15 February 2009.

Butler, J. (2004) *Precarious Life: The powers of mourning and violence*. London: Verso.

Butler, J. (2005) *Giving an Account of Oneself*. New York: Fordham University Press.

Ceppi, G. and Zini, M. (eds) (1998) *Children, Spaces, Relations: Metaproject for an environment for young children*. Milan: Domus Academy Research Center.

Colebrook, C. (2002) *Gilles Deleuze*. London: Routledge.

Dahlberg, G. and Moss, P. (2005) *Ethics and Politics in Early Childhood Education*. London: Routledge/Falmer.

Davies, B. (2005) "The Fairy Who Wouldn't Fly: A story of subjection and agency". *Journal of Early Childhood Literacy* 5(2): 151–174.

Davies, B. (2008) "Re-thinking 'behaviour' in terms of positioning and the ethics of responsibility". In A. M. Phelan and J. Sumsion (eds), *Critical Readings in Teacher Education: Provoking absences*. Netherlands: Sense Publishers, pp. 173–186.

Davies, B. (2009a) "Life in Kings Cross: A play of voices". In A. Jackson and L. Mazzei (eds), *Voice in Qualitative Inquiry: Challenging conventional, interpretive and critical conceptions in qualitative research*. New York: Routledge, pp. 197–220.

Davies, B. (2009b) "Difference and differentiation". In B. Davies and S. Gannon (eds), *Pedagogical Encounters*. New York: Peter Lang.

Davies, B. (2010) "The implications for qualitative research methodology of the struggle between the individualized subject of phenomenology and the emergent multiplicities of the poststructuralist subject: The problem of agency". *Reconceptualizing Education Research Methodology* 1(1): 54–68.

Davies, B. and Bansel, P. (2005) "The time of their lives? Academic workers in neoliberal time(s)". *Health Sociology Review* 14(1): 47–58.

Davies, B. and Bansel, P. (2007a) "Neoliberalism and education". *International Journal of Qualitative Studies in Education.* Special issue on neoliberalism and education edited by Bronwyn Davies and Peter Bansel 20(3): 247–260.

Davies, B. and Bansel, P. (2007b) "Governmentality and academic work: Shaping the hearts and minds of academic workers". *Journal of Curriculum Theorizing* July 23(2): 9–26.

Davies, B. and Gannon, S. (2006) *Doing Collective Biography*. Maidenhead: Open University Press, pp. 1–200.

Davies, B. and Gannon, S. (eds) (2009) *Pedagogical Encounters*. New York: Routledge.

Davies, B. and Gannon, S. (2013) "Collective biography and the entangled enlivening of being". *International Review of Qualitative Research* 5(4): 357–376.

Davies, B. and Harré, R. (1990) "Positioning: The discursive production of selves". *Journal for the Theory of Social Behaviour* 20(1): 43–63.

Davies, B., Browne, J., Gannon, S., Honan, E., Laws, C., Mueller-Rockstroh, B. and Bendix Petersen, E. (2004) "The ambivalent practices of reflexivity". *Qualitative Inquiry* 10(2): 360–390.

Davies, B., De Schauwer, E., Claes, L., De Munck, K., De Schauwer, E., Van De Putte, I. and Verstichele, M. (2013) "Recognition and difference: A collective biography". *International Journal of Qualitative Studies in Education* 26(6): 680–690.

Deleuze, G. (1980) "Cours Vincennes 12/21/1980". Available online: http://www.webdeleuze.com/php/texte.php?cle=190andgroupe=Spinozaandlangue=2(accessed 10 February 2010).

Deleuze, G. (1988) *Spinoza: Practical philosophy* (trans. R. Hurley). San Francisco, CA: City Lights Books.

Deleuze, G. (1990) *The Logic of Sense*. New York: Columbia University Press.

Deleuze, G. (1994) *Difference and Repetition*. London: Continuum.

Deleuze, G. (1995) *Negotiations 1972–1990* (trans. M. Joughin). New York: Columbia University Press.

Deleuze, G. (1997) "To have done with judgment". In G. Deleuze, *Essays Critical and Clinical* (trans. D. W. Smith and M. A. Greco). Minneapolis, MN: University of Minnesota Press, pp. 126–135.

Deleuze, G. and Guattari, F. (1987) *A Thousand Plateaus: Capitalism and schizophrenia*. London: Athlone Press.

Deleuze, G. and Guattari, F. (1994) *What Is Philosophy?* New York: Columbia University Press.

Deleuze, G. and Parnet, C. (1987) *Dialogues*. New York: Columbia University Press.

Hallward, P. (2002) "Translator's introduction". In A. Badiou, *Ethics: An essay on the understanding of evil*. London: Verso, pp. vii–xlvii.

Halsey, M. (2007) "Molar ecology: What can the (full) body of an eco-tourist do?" In A. Hickey-Moody and P. Malins (eds), *Deleuzian Encounters: Studies in contemporary social issues*. Basingstoke: Palgrave Macmillan, pp. 135–150.

Herrigal, E. (1953) *Zen in the Art of Archery*. New York: Pantheon.

Hultman, K. and Lenz Taguchi, H. (2010) "Challenging anthropocentric analysis of visual data: A relational materialist methodological approach to educational research". *International Journal of Qualitative Studies in Education* 23(5): 525–542.

Kumashiro, K. (2008) *The Seduction of Common Sense: How the Right has framed the debate on America's schools*. New York: Teachers College Press.

Latour, B. (1999) *Pandora's Hope: Essays on the reality of science studies.* Cambridge, MA: Harvard University Press.

Laws, C. (2011) *Rethinking Research and Professional Practices in Terms of Relationality, Subjectivity and Power: Poststructuralism at work with marginalised children.* UAE: Bentham Science Publications.

Laws, C. and Davies, B. (2000) "Poststructuralist theory in practice: Working with 'behaviourally disturbed' children". *International Journal of Qualitative Studies in Education* 13(3): 205–221.

Lehrer, J. (2007) *Proust Was a Neuroscientist.* Boston, MA: Houghton Mifflin Company.

Lenz Taguchi, H. (2010) *Going Beyond the Theory/Practice Divide in Early Childhood Education: Introducing an intra-active pedagogy.* London: Routledge/Falmer.

Lenz Taguchi, H. (2012) "A diffractive and Deleuzian approach to analyzing interview data". *Feminist Theory* 13(3): 265–281.

Lenz Taguchi, H. and Palmer, A. (2013) "A more 'livable' school? A diffractive analysis of the performative enactments of girls' ill-/well-being with(in) school environments". *Gender and Education* 25(6): 671–687.

Linnell, S. (2010) *Art Psychotherapy and Narrative Therapy: An account of practitioner research.* UAE: Bentham Science e-books.

Massey, D. (2005) *For Space.* London: Sage Publications.

Nancy, J.-L. (2007) *Listening* (trans. C. Mandell). New York: Fordham University Press.

O'Harris, P. (1945) *The Fairy Who Wouldn't Fly.* Sydney: Marchant.

O'Harris, P. (retold by David Harris) (1974) *The Fairy Who Wouldn't Fly.* Sydney: Angus and Robertson.

O'Harris, P. (retold by Bronwyn Davies) (2014) *The Fairy Who Wouldn't Fly.* Canberra: Australian National Library.

Readings, B. (1996) *The University in Ruins.* Cambridge, MA: Harvard University Press.

Rinaldi, C. (2006) *In Dialogue with Reggio Emilia: Listening, researching and learning.* London: Routledge.

Roffe, J. (2007) "Politics beyond identity". In A. Hickey-Moody and P. Malins (eds), *Deleuzian Encounters: Studies in contemporary social issues.* Basingstoke: Palgrave Macmillan, pp. 40–49.

Schulte, C. M. (2013) "Being there and becoming-unfaithful". *International Journal of Education & the Arts*, 14(SI 1.5). Available online: http://www.ijea.org/v14si1/ (accessed on 10 October 2013).

Silver, G. and Krömer, C. (2009) *Anh's Anger.* Berkeley, CA: Plum Blossom Books.

Somerville, M., Davies, B., Power, K., Gannon, S. and de Carteret, P. (2011) *Place Pedagogy Change.* Netherlands: Sense Publishers.

Søndergaard, D. M. (2012) "Bullying and social exclusion anxiety in schools". *British Journal of Sociology of Education* 34: 1–18.

Taubman, P. M. (2010) "Alain Badiou, Jacques Lacan and the ethics of teaching". *Educational Philosophy and Theory* 42(2): 196–212.

Thich Nhat Hanh (1998) *Interbeing: Fourteen Guidelines for Engaged Buddhism* (3rd edn). Berkeley, CA: Parallax Press.

Thich Nhat Hanh (2001) *Anger: Wisdom for cooling the flames.* New York: Riverhead Books.

Thich Nhat Hanh (2010) *This Sun My Heart*. Berkeley, CA: Parallax Press.

Venn, C. (2002) "Refiguring subjectivity after modernity". In V. Walkerdine (ed.), *Challenging Subjects: Critical psychology for a new millennium*. Basingstoke: Palgrave Macmillan, pp. 51–71.

Watts, A. (1957) *The Way of Zen*. New York: Vintage Books.

Williams, J. (2003) *Gilles Deleuze's Difference and Repetition*. Edinburgh: Edinburgh University Press.

Wilson, E. A. (2004) *Psychosomatic: Feminism and the neurological body*. Durham, NC: Duke University Press.

Woolf, V. (1978) *Moments of Being*. Reading: Triad/Granada.

Index

#0319 - 031016 - C16 - 234/156/8 - PB - 9781138780903